T0226007

Unlocking Blockchain on Azure

Design and Develop Decentralized Applications

Shilpa Karkeraa

Apress®

Unlocking Blockchain on Azure: Design and Develop Decentralized Applications

Shilpa Karkeraa
Mumbai, India

ISBN-13 (pbk): 978-1-4842-5042-6   ISBN-13 (electronic): 978-1-4842-5043-3
https://doi.org/10.1007/978-1-4842-5043-3

Copyright © 2020 by Shilpa Karkeraa

This work is subject to copyright. All rights are reserved by the Publisher, whether the whole or part of the material is concerned, specifically the rights of translation, reprinting, reuse of illustrations, recitation, broadcasting, reproduction on microfilms or in any other physical way, and transmission or information storage and retrieval, electronic adaptation, computer software, or by similar or dissimilar methodology now known or hereafter developed.

Trademarked names, logos, and images may appear in this book. Rather than use a trademark symbol with every occurrence of a trademarked name, logo, or image, we use the names, logos, and images only in an editorial fashion and to the benefit of the trademark owner, with no intention of infringement of the trademark.

The use in this publication of trade names, trademarks, service marks, and similar terms, even if they are not identified as such, is not to be taken as an expression of opinion as to whether or not they are subject to proprietary rights.

While the advice and information in this book are believed to be true and accurate at the date of publication, neither the authors nor the editors nor the publisher can accept any legal responsibility for any errors or omissions that may be made. The publisher makes no warranty, express or implied, with respect to the material contained herein.

Managing Director, Apress Media LLC: Welmoed Spahr
Acquisitions Editor: Smriti Srivastava
Development Editor: Matthew Moodie
Coordinating Editor: Shrikant Vishwakarma

Cover designed by eStudioCalamar

Cover image designed by Freepik (www.freepik.com)

Distributed to the book trade worldwide by Springer Science+Business Media New York, 233 Spring Street, 6th Floor, New York, NY 10013. Phone 1-800-SPRINGER, fax (201) 348-4505, email orders-ny@springer-sbm.com, or visit www.springeronline.com. Apress Media, LLC is a California LLC and the sole member (owner) is Springer Science+Business Media Finance Inc (SSBM Finance Inc). SSBM Finance Inc is a **Delaware** corporation.

For information on translations, please email rights@apress.com or visit http://www.apress.com/rights-permissions.

Apress titles may be purchased in bulk for academic, corporate, or promotional use. eBook versions and licenses are also available for most titles. For more information, reference our Print and eBook Bulk Sales web page at http://www.apress.com/bulk-sales.

Any source code or other supplementary material referenced by the author in this book is available to readers on GitHub via the book's product page, located at www.apress.com/978-1-4842-5042-6. For more-detailed information, please visit http://www.apress.com/source-code.

Printed on acid-free paper

*Dedicated to every active node in this
open ecosystem that triggers sparks, igniting
every mind toward making this world a better
place to live!*

Table of Contents

About the Author

Shilpa Karkeraa is the leading AI technology expert and the CEO and founder of Myraa Technologies. She is an IIM Bangalore Scholar with Goldman Sachs Recognition, and her roots in electronics and telecom engineering originate from the University of Pune. She has been awarded Best CIO for Digital Transformation by the Computer Society of India. Besides catering to nine diverse industries, she is a strategic technology advisor to several companies worldwide.

A serial entrepreneur with more than twenty-five large-scale deployments, she has nurtured a team of passionate innovators to build state-of-the-art voice models, trading engines, and cognitive AI apps used by over a million users. Solving global industrial challenges in India, the UK, Europe, and Singapore, she has created a high learning curve research ecosystem.

Prior to Myraa, she worked as a team lead–data engineering group of a Bay Area startup, lead technologist with top corporate financial service firms, and as a principal architect at a Singaporean B2C company. She was also CTO and technology advisor to several new-age companies.

She is an active global technology speaker. She envisions commercializing research and innovation to touch human lives effectively!

Acknowledgments

Writing this book has been a roller coaster of hands-on developments, interactions, explorations, and validations from diverse areas of the globe with respect to industries, sectors, locations, and so forth. I thank every person I have met on this journey who helped me envision a decentralized ecosystem with blockchains.

I express my gratitude toward the opportunity to share my experiences on the subject and the trust extended to me by the acquisition editor, Smriti Srivastava, and her team at Apress Media. I am thankful to the technical reviewer, Jean-Luc Verhelst, for his valuable constructive feedback on the subject, and to Matthew Moodie for all the editorial clarity to make the book more comprehensible.

Further, I truly appreciate the support my researchers at Myraa Technologies extended regarding technological developments in the book and the use cases. I appreciate my partners in several entrepreneurial initiatives to nurture a decentralized ecosystem.

I am grateful for all the creative juices from Shashwath Bolar regarding the concept and implementation of the design of this book. I am thankful for Rhythm Jolly from Aditya Birla Capital for his review and feedback on how to make the concepts in this book more relatable for the everyday reader.

Lastly, I thank the gems of my life—dear Mum & Dad: Usha Karkera and Shashikant M. Karkera—for their unconditional love and support throughout! My mother's compassionate fighting spirit to overcome challenges in life and my father's passionate advice, both of which I inherited, make the writings in this book truly an experience!

Introduction

Unlocking Blockchain on Azure walks through the different layers of understanding blockchains, from defining them in several contexts to deploying them in Enterprise environments. This book aims to unfold all the aspects in and around blockchains in the most comprehensible ways. The book envisions demystifying concepts, processes, and the usability of blockchains in diverse industries, such as supply chain, manufacturing, maritime, oil and gas, trade finance, and many more.

Structure of the Book

The first three chapters define blockchains and their components. They provide examples and use cases throughout to maintain relatability for readers from all domains. They aim to cover the breadth and depth of the concept. These chapters introduce the Azure Blockchain Workbench and its capabilities that leverage the infrastructure tools.

The second set of three chapters explores things both internal and external to the decentralized platform. Here, the focus is on business developers and solution architects to help them make and interpret suitable decisions for their applications. These chapters make one aware of how to plan better for one's business requirements and help one draft a better plan for development.

Lastly, the final set of chapters open up an array of technological tools and architectures that may be considered based on the application. The book guides one to make decisions that lead to a truly decentralized process. It has a lot of use cases in store as you read the book. The book closes with hands-on exercises to review the chapters and their implementations.

What You'll Learn

- Understanding what Azure Blockchain Service enables and its components from various perspectives and industries

- Learn to design decentralized applications with the design guide of Azure Blockchain Service

- Drive processes and operations through a transparent, decentralized platform with several configurations of setup based on requirements

- Accelerate processes with automated smart contracts

- Develop decentralized applications

Who This Book Is For

- Business Developers: Who envision improving business processes

- Solution Architects: For architecting decentralized platforms such that isolated system setups talk to each other in a transparent connected network

- Developers: To understand technological tools and DevOps with Azure Blockchain Service

The source code and images can be found at the following:

www.myraatechnologies.com/unlocking-blockchains-with-azure

CHAPTER 1

Blockchains: The Complete Picture

This chapter breaks down every aspect of blockchains in a simplistic way, unlocking the barriers of technical know-how and opening up avenues for other domain experiences to blend with the infrastructure provided by blockchains. Thereby enabling users both with and without the infrastructure to use Microsoft Azure with Blockchains to make a decentralized lifestyle truly happen in all walks of life!

So, whether you are an academician, CIO, people operation strategist, mechanical engineer, architect, or even a ten-year-old, or if you feel like one, I envision that you can build your understanding block by block in this chapter. Further, from this chapter, we move toward real-life blockchain deployments and how we can develop them to fit every individual aspect of the blockchain and its variants available.

We shall see how blockchains are changing the ways in which we deal with money and the economics around it. Once the foundation of blockchains is set, we will learn about smart contracts, which enable users to experience digital contracts that trigger actions programmatically and enforce pre-agreed-upon clauses. From there, we will discover the integration of the external world of existing software with blockchains in the Enterprise, which requires large-scale movements. Toward Chapter 7, we will open up the array of tools that are available to form blockchain policies, business design, architecture, and development tools.

© Shilpa Karkeraa 2020
S. Karkeraa, *Unlocking Blockchain on Azure*,
https://doi.org/10.1007/978-1-4842-5043-3_1

Knowing that this book will be read by people from diverse backgrounds, we will elaborate different cases of technical architectures used to build blockchain platforms and DApps (decentralized applications). We will broaden our understanding with use cases from all over the world in diverse fields and explore inter-disciplinary integrations of blockchains.

Now that we have previewed the ocean of things that are going to be coming in the next couple of chapters, let's focus on why we might use blockchains. What makes them so popular, and why do they promise to change the ways of money, business, and the world? Why are more than 50 percent of the world's largest digital companies invested in this technology? This is what many individuals, companies, and ecosystems wish to understand. However, on a day-to-day basis, how do blockchains affect you? In what way do your surroundings change with this technology? How would you interact with blockchains?

All these answers will unfold in this chapter and in the course of this book.

Like the 6 Sigma transition, across the five stages of define, measure, analyze, improve, and control over any challenge that improves yield stage by stage, this chapter brings the following six transitions:

- Introduction – Defining blockchains

- Benchmarking – Historical events of evolution to modern-day blockchains

- Measuring the change from distributed computing to distributed ledgers

- Analyzing the impact and improvement with blockchains in action

- Control decentralization with consensus

- Implement with Azure and scale across

Defining Blockchains

Humans best understand the world through exploration and discovery. Humans group together into an ecosystem to get life moving. Businesses form communities, supply chains, and economies within countries and across borders. The true nature of connecting, interacting, and evolving is at the core of everything in existence.

Blockchains bring this very form of interaction, connectivity, and evolution to a software platform. They digitize not just data, but also the processes and the state of the processes in a digital ledger. Blockchains are a form of distributed digital ledger that doesn't just hold data but also interacts with the daily operations of life.

Blockchains represent a chain of blocks. This chain is a connected network of people interacting with one another in the form of blocks of data. That sounds like an existing social network, like Facebook, Instagram, Twitter, or others that we all know of. So, how is a blockchain different? In any existing social media platform or service, the user data is stored, transferred, and managed by a centralized server hosted and governed by the social media platform itself. If the platform were to be on a blockchain, that same user data would be stored, transacted, and governed in the form of blocks of data hosted and distributed by the end users themselves and not a single company. This is how blockchains enable end users to have better control of their data and its privacy, and to have awareness of how their data is stored, maintained, and distributed.

A blockchain enables a group of users to come to an agreement on any action, transaction, or decision based on a pre-defined set of rules. It allows everyone into the decision-making process. Further, it empowers the chain's complete right to privacy with its encryption of the data blocks and transactions.

So far, we have understood blockchains to be a chain of blocks connected between peer-to-peer networks. Those blocks are hosted by peers themselves and are connected by the principle of consensus agreements over encrypted data and direct transactions. From there, a blockchain provides an avenue to digitize the efforts, value, and representation of money on that chain as it forms the single source of trusted truth.

Further on, we will see the definition of a blockchain from a beginner's perspective, and then an expert's understanding, noting the varied levels of complexity and technicality.

Defining for a New User

If you are someone entirely new to the concept of blockchains or have just begun your journey in understanding and building blockchains, the following example might help you visualize an actual trade performed via blockchain. Before blockchains, the process went as shown in Figure 1-1.

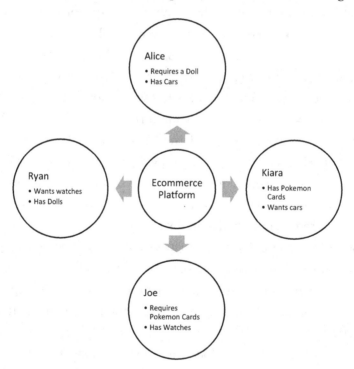

Figure 1-1. *Centralized system where trade happens only through the shop*

As seen in Figure 1-1, Alice, Ryan, Kiara, and Joe all transact over the e-commerce platform to either purchase or sell goods. This e-commerce platform may charge them a commission every time they transact and may regulate the prices as per its own policies.

However, all of them trust the platform brand to transact and execute deals with unknown users globally. Thus, they are relying on a centralized, single source of trust.

When Alice, Ryan, Kiara, and Joe are on a blockchain, however, it goes as shown in Figure 1-2.

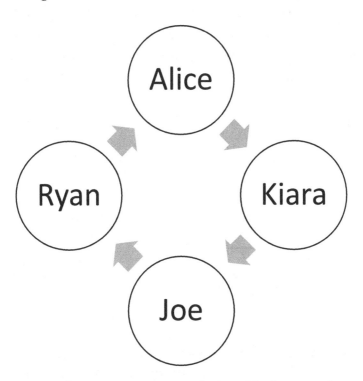

Figure 1-2. *Trade peer-to-peer on a chain with the agreed-upon value, with not one single intermediary but rather a chain of people to validate the transaction*

They all can barter or trade or exchange items directly and have no loss of value or trust issues. The trust is maintained, witnessed by others who validate the trade. As we see in Figure 1-2, when Alice purchases from Ryan, the network of Kiara and Joe becomes a witness of the trade; likewise while others trade. This chain could have infinite people, and a voting majority can allow the transaction on a chain.

Defining for a Beginner

Now that you understand the basic premise of blockchains, we will explore a case with a higher amount of complexity in the transaction. Before blockchains, data stored by the intermediary may or may not be tampered with or credible (Figure 1-3).

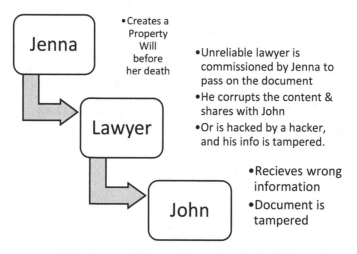

Figure 1-3. *Use case where multiple parties are involved via a contract, and the credibility may be questionable due to the intermediary involved*

As we see in Figure 1-3, Jenna creates a property will and entrusts it to her lawyer to rightfully execute after her death. However, the will may be vulnerable to changes resulting from any tampering or manhandling done by someone with malicious or biased intent. This can result in an unfair transaction, which may not always be traceable and can impact someone like John in a negative manner, as we can see in the transaction in Figure 1-4.

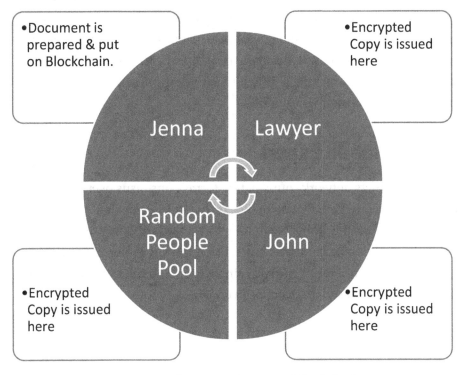

Figure 1-4. *Tamper-proof transaction on a blockchains*

After using a blockchain, you get a transaction like that in Figure 1-4. The encrypted copy of the will is available to everyone involved in the transaction. However, modifying the document would require consensus from everyone on the blockchain, thus preventing any changes to the will without everyone approving it.

The lawyer or other peer cannot modify the document without an update being sent alerting all parties involved in the consensus. John thus receives a tamper-proof document. Any hacker on the chain cannot mess with the data on the chain in a single instance of hacking. He'd have to have voting rights across the chain to change the document across all copies on the chain, making it difficult to attack the document. This makes the data on a blockchain immutable.

Defining for an Expert

Figure 1-5 depicts network software that forms consensus over an end-to-end encrypted chain of blocks that links peers that are distributed across the globe, facilitating direct trade and transactions with a centralized intermediary, but a decentralized witness system. The ownership of control is not with any single user. The validation control is also randomized based on the chosen consensus protocol.

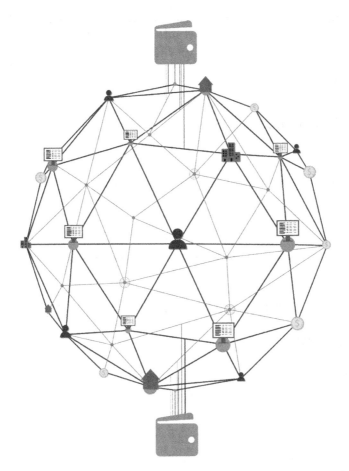

Figure 1-5. *Users, devices, data, and transactions connected in a network forming a blockchain*

To understand the concepts that are basic to building any blockchain application/service, let us review the key elements of transparency, encryption, immutability, decentralization, and privacy with the exercise below.

EXERCISE: THINK AND SKETCH CHAIN VIEW OF BLOCKCHAIN IN DIFFERENT ENVIRONMENTS

1. Food we eat

2. Money we trade

3. Documents we share

4. Purchases we make

5. People we trust and engage in relations

6. Companies we deal with

Historical Chain of Events: Distributed Computing

In the olden days of bartering in trade, people used to exchange goods and services based on their own understanding of the value behind a particular barter. This value was situational and was not entirely standardized. People were free to equate a bar of gold with 100 kgs of rice or five acres of land based on their own understanding of the demand and supply. From there, the concept of value started becoming centralized when those in power standardized the value of goods against the currency issued. From that currency, nations evolved to have their own currencies. The relative value of one currency to another depended on the world's trade and countries' dependency on one another. So any currency is simply a form of value trusted by all based on the declaration of a centralized authority. Now that we are digitizing currency, effort, and value, one may vary the value of currency to the digital quantification. Therefore, money is simply a form of data trusted and accepted by consensus; the value cannot be changed by anybody but the centralized authority. On the other hand, having data on blockchains provides a decentralized acceptance of a value locked on the chain that is immutable and unchangeable on the shared ledger. This brings a promise of performing value-based trades directly across groups of people in different sectors, countries, and experiences on a connected network without any centralized authority; there is simply a group of decentralized people across the chain adding validation.

Now that we understand the evolution of trust-based value, let us see how we grew technologically across networks. In the dot-com boom, several centralized platforms emerged as aggregators over the internet. These aggregators opened up the world to trade through themselves. For example, eBay, Amazon, and Alibaba all enable people to purchase items through their platforms that are not locally sold or available. The policies on these platforms are governed by the platform holders themselves. The subscribers to such platforms simply rely on the trust and brand value they hold. So, every time you put your credit card details onto such a portal, you are trusting that centralized entity to facilitate trade. On the technology side of it, the credit card details are encrypted by the centralized platform via mechanisms chosen by that centralized platform. This is not transparent to the user, and it will never be known if it is fully secure or not.

On other hand, various blockchain platforms open up what their source code does and showcase the root of trust to be the dynamic end-to-end encryptions that are under the full control of the end user. So, unlike trusting the centralized platform, you trust the network, which does not represent one single company.

With the advancements in computing devices over the past decades (as seen in Figure 1-6), their scalability, adaptability, and affordability suited large-scale consumers across the world—so much so that 5.13 billion people (about 66 percent of the world's population) have computing devices in the form of mobile phones, computers, and Internet of Things (IoT) devices, as per Global System for Mobile Communications (GSMA) real-time intelligence data. We are now more connected than ever before, via high-speed compact devices that we carry with us. Our digital traces are already everywhere. However, with this growing rate of digital use, we leave traces of ourselves leaking all over the internet, vulnerable to attacks and security breaches and exhibiting a pitiful state of trust in brands that showcase value but do not entirely take responsibility for our data.

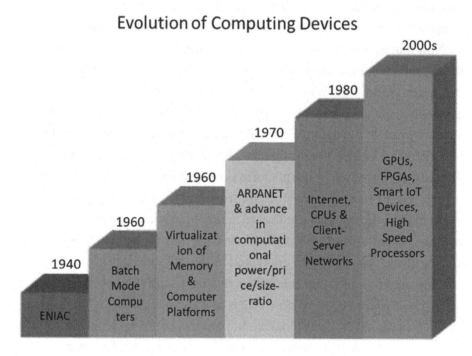

Figure 1-6. *Evolution of computing devices*

The applications we use currently online on a day to day basis, provide us only with the front end or the outer facade to use the application, and we have very little to no control over the centralized platforms used by these applications in the backend that define and govern the usage of the platform and the data we generate on it. The previous era found us highly engaged in social networks, trade networks, e-commerce networks, and so on. We all have been subscribers or clients of several centrally hosted digital services. All of these were secured with a simple password that stopped the neighbor from logging in.

With digitization, the pattern of interaction between a consumer and a company is more online, creating a need for different business models and also leading to business online. Similarly, hackers have gotten more sophisticated, with improved computing devices to guess your passwords, hack systems, extract data, and manipulate transactions every day. Over 40,000 websites get hacked daily.

Our current form of digital network surely needs to evolve. Thereby blockchains.

Let's examine what this change of network styles looks like for every type of consumer.

Stage 1: Client-Server

Subscribers use a hosted server service for its facilities (see Figure 1-7). A lot of our search engines, e-commerce platforms, and websites started with this.

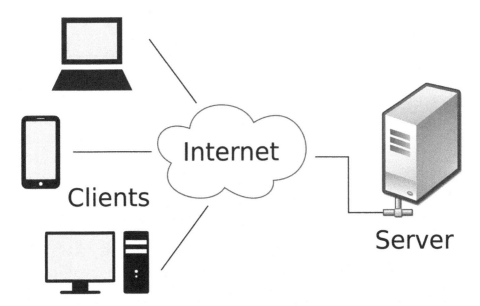

Figure 1-7. *The client-server model*

Most of the logic, data, and user interface pages are hosted on a single server.

As computing devices evolved and the user base grew, businesses started multi-tiering their network architecture. For example, if 10,000 users/clients wished to access the same server at the same time in the traditional client-server network architecture, the loading time of a website could be really long. Thereby, Stage 2 evolved.

Stage 2: Multi-tier Network Architecture

Here, the client-side logic was separate, the intermediate layers of memory computation and calculations were separate, and the database had data logging and data storage facilities maintained separately (as shown in Figure 1-8). For example, trading engines, banking applications, email services, and so forth are multi-tiered.

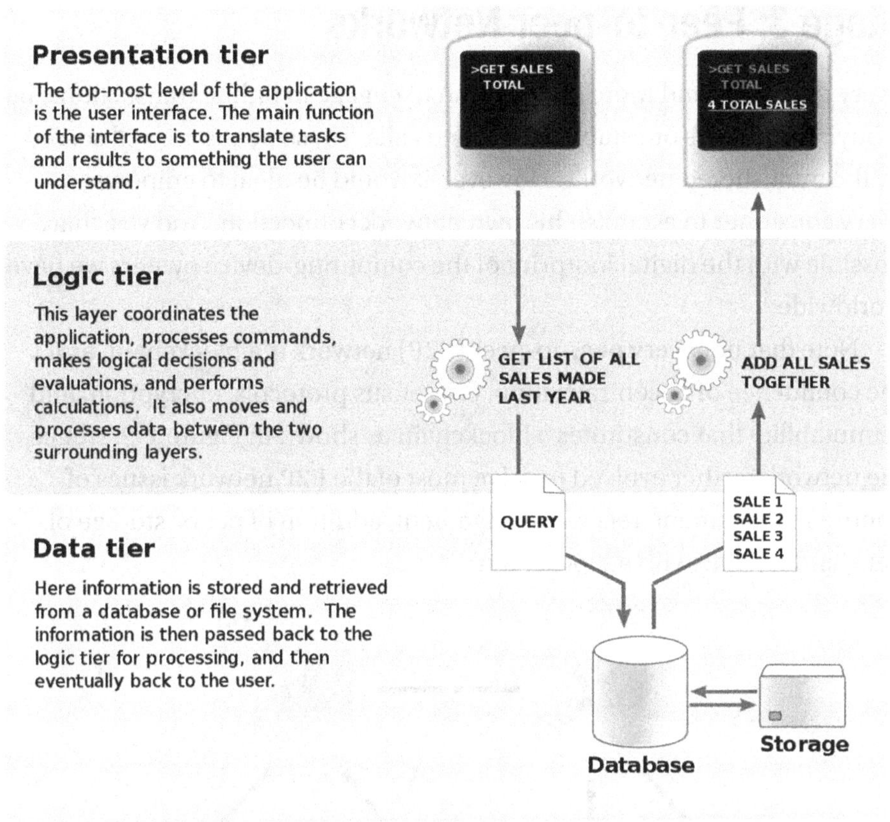

Presentation tier

The top-most level of the application is the user interface. The main function of the interface is to translate tasks and results to something the user can understand.

>GET SALES
TOTAL

>GET SALES
TOTAL
4 TOTAL SALES

Logic tier

This layer coordinates the application, processes commands, makes logical decisions and evaluations, and performs calculations. It also moves and processes data between the two surrounding layers.

GET LIST OF ALL
SALES MADE
LAST YEAR

ADD ALL SALES
TOGETHER

QUERY

SALE 1
SALE 2
SALE 3
SALE 4

Data tier

Here information is stored and retrieved from a database or file system. The information is then passed back to the logic tier for processing, and then eventually back to the user.

Storage
Database

Figure 1-8. *Multi-tier network architecture*

We now understand the limitations of a centrally hosted set of servers that result from its issues with data privacy, storage, and network structure. The third stage brings us a fully connected mesh of servers that work peer-to-peer. A server is nothing but a machine that hosts services on its own for others to access based on desired permissions set by the machine itself. Your very own mobile phone or tablet can be a server. Thereby, the evolution of Stage 3.

Stage 3: Peer-to-peer Networks

Every day, more and more people wish to engage in online transactions, be it buying groceries or establishing video calls. These needs are still served by the multi-tiered networks. However, it would be ideal to empower every consumer to establish his own network connection. And yes, that's possible with the digital footprint of the computing-device owners we have worldwide.

Note that not every peer-to-peer (P2P) network is a blockchain, as it's the confluence of decentralization, consensus protocols, encryption, and immutability that constitutes a blockchain as shown in Figure 1-9. Hence, the network further evolved to solve most of the P2P network issues of control management, record management, addition of peers, storage of data, and its state with a blockchain.

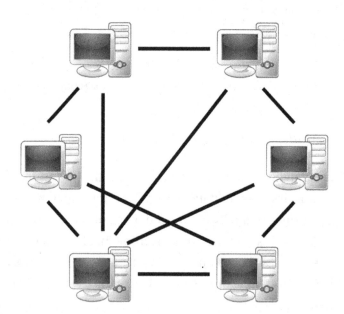

Figure 1-9. *A peer-to-peer network*

Every user today with a mobile phone, tablet, computer, or IoT device (known as edge devices) can be a peer in this connected network. With the advancements of virtualization and cloud computing, services to use a cloud-based instance extend to any user. So, if your laptop or edge device does not have the computational capacity to interact with a large connected network for blockchain-based transactions, Azure provides the infrastructure to form a peer node in a blockchain.

Azure's Blockchain Workbench not only allows you to participate as a peer node, but also empowers users to form a connected network using any blockchain framework. In the coming chapters, you shall see the infrastructure enablers offered by Azure to onboard your offline or centralized online network to a true decentralized blockchain network.

So from a Community Manager in one part of the globe to any wanderer in the extreme far away lands could connect over Blockchains with Azure, combining the trust & decentralization from Blockchains & Cloud computing facilities by Azure.

In simple terms, Azure's Blockchain Workbench allows anyone to set up the components of a blockchain environment with just a couple of clicks. It lets you initialize the components required to set up such a blockchain network.

Stage 4: Blockchain

With this, we are now ready to empower every user in a peer-to-peer network to be aware of, engage with, and deal over such a secure network through blockchains. So now, if you find yourself buying vegetables over a blockchain, the blockchain allows you to know the following:

- How it grew
- The entire traceability of where it came from

- Which distributor packaged it

- Who shipped it

- Who gets paid with it

The following questions may arise regarding this activity that could take place over any e-commerce website:

- Why would I want to know?

- Why can't the e-commerce website mention these facts?

- Why do I care who gets paid as long as I receive it?

The answers to this lie in the frustration of having zero control over the following:

- The quality that is delivered (they say some plants are grown by the drainage)

- The e-commerce platform may manipulate facts or glorify information.

- The harmful toxic packaging it may come in

- An inefficient supply chain trade makes it expensive

- Shipping goes rogue at times

- Payments are deducted in advance by your card companies, and it sometimes does not reach the retailer (used to happen in the early days of online payments).

Blockchains enable the following:

- Full transparency with complete credibility of data from real end user providing it

- True validation with a network of peers as a decentralized form of authority

- A mature network of consensus and policies formed and accepted by all

- Tamper-proof data on a shared ledger with public and private chain options

- A true source of immutable truth

- Highly secure end-to-end encryption for confidential data with anonymity maintained wherever required

- Automated contracts that are mutually developed, accepted, enforced, and executed

- A clearer form of quantification of value that can be transacted with no enforced centralized intermediary.

Let's look at one more example here of a real-life situation where our digital networks of human interaction need to mature for better quality of life: building construction.

Millions of dollars' worth of life savings are heavily invested by homeowners so they can have a decent form of shelter and a real estate property with the goal of achieving long-term returns. So, when you buy a house, what steps do you take?

1. Search locations that are suitable.

2. Configurations that are in budget

3. Structures that are desirable

4. Builders that are reliable or brand-worthy

5. Architects who construct well and maintain quality and strength

6. Suppliers who provide the best raw materials

7. Housing developers who construct it to the requirements

All these steps rely on trust that is developed based on the past experiences of these professionals. Now, imagine if this entire manual screening of hunting for a property were taken onto a blockchain. It would allow the home buyers to know and engage in the following:

- Where did the cement and other raw materials come from?

- Which college did the architect go to, and is he authorized for the desired structure?

- Which licenses does the builder have?

- Is it really the landowner you are genuinely dealing with?

- Are all documents genuine from the true source?

- Provide a digital signature that will be witnessed by the peer network

The information behind all the questions above, is pulled out from a different network of peers that would be hosting that particular information and provided to prospective home buyers directly in a blockchain scenario. Compare this to the traditional one-spot trust of the housing developers or builders.

This is the perspective from the solo-user angle. However, while visualizing the perks of such a transparent open-loop network, users often worry about putting everything out there digitally. This worry is handled via the blockchain variants of public and private blockchains. The network is usually a consortium or a hybrid mesh of public and private blockchains. In such a network, peers are selectively added on a private network, whereas a public blockchain network opens itself up to a larger audience and handles general information.

So, in an e-commerce blockchain network, the following aspects may be considered while designing a blockchain:

- The public blockchain could have a general listing of products, as on a centralized platform.

    a. However, this data is immutable or tamper-proof.

    b. All states and transitions will permanently be a part of the public blockchain.

    c. The validation of sources may be verified by existing peers by a common form of principle (consensus).

    d. The onboarding of product suppliers can be done directly on the chain without a centralized authority approving it, but a group of peers must validate the onboarding.

    e. For any change of information by the product supplier, all peers or most peers have to agree and accept so as to have all copies of the peer network contain the same information.

- The private blockchain could handle the transaction privately, in terms of information about what was purchased and who purchased it, all of which can be transferred between the involved parties directly.

    a. The peers in the private blockchain could still allow/validate the transfer of encrypted data packets based on the pre-agreed consensus.

    b.   The private details are encrypted end-to-end with the public key and decrypted with the private key. The key management can be of various configurations, as explained in Chapter 3 under "Encryptions."

    c.   In case of a resell, the new buyer could be added to this very private chain to trace the purchase history and the true source of the document and digital trail.

Similarly, for a home buyer, the following transactions are suited for public and private blockchains chains:

Public Blockchains	Private Blockchains
Listing records of developers' products and services	Quotation for purchase
Past records of developments	Transaction of the deal
Reviews and experiences of past customers	Digital signature of agreement
Listing of architect's portfolio	Smart contract over clauses
Sources of raw material	Buy/sell /resell
Land history	Mortgages/loans, if any
Licenses and certificates	
Delivery status and completion rates	

Remember: all of these can always be done on a centralized platform. There are several existing ways to solve problems that cause mistrust. However, these platforms are not transparent. They don't let you engage with the true source of information. They don't let the source reach you directly. Does that really mean that intermediaries are out of business?

No, they are given a more open avenue to connect people more transparently to a fair market across the globe.

Now that we've reviewed the variants of blockchains and their actual impact, let's examine the key terminology that matters while working with them.

Blockchain Terminology

Technical definition of blockchain:

- A blockchain can be defined as an append-only list of blocks that are stored in a decentralized form of storage across a peer-to-peer network and encrypted using cryptography, and that exist under a common principal of agreement whereby the network majority verifies the transactions on the chain.

The definitions of jargonistic words are broken down as follows:

Jargon	Simple words
Append-only	Adds every single state of the record. Once added, cannot be removed.
Blocks	Records of transaction information that is encrypted into a hash and encoded into a Merkle tree.
Hash	A **hash** is a function that converts an input of letters and numbers into an encrypted output of a fixed length.
Encrypt	To convert (information or data) into a code, especially to prevent unauthorized access
Cryptography	Study of techniques for secure communication in the presence of third parties

(*continued*)

Jargon	Simple words
Consensus	A common form of agreement by all/majority
Distributed	Not stored in a single or centralized source, making it less vulnerable for crackers/hackers
Trust	A computationally developed method of reliability
Merkle tree	A form of data structure that ensures blocks are verifiable efficiently and securely

Here is what really happens:

1. A piece of data is broken down into hashed blocks.

2. A network is formed by several devices (peers) connected in a chain form.

3. The network forms a general rule of common consensus.

4. Consensus can be of various types, such as one based on work that happened, ownership that is involved, or various voting mechanisms that are commonly agreed upon.

5. Blocks of data are transferred to this network such that all devices get updated with the information upon approval by a network majority consensus based on the rule.

6. Once transferred, this block cannot be independently tampered with by anyone unless all blocks are updated with a new change, which will be an additional block of data.

7. The existing block does not change at any cost.

8. The energy spent in this transfer, validation, and storage is the true value cost of the transaction.

This illustration varies in several ways based on the vision of the blockchain and the purpose it wishes to serve its users. For example, if the blockchain is for verifying identities, then the method of consensus will vary along with the treatment of data and the process of operation involved.

However, the foundation of decentralization remains constant. The other variables' ratios vary based on the peer configurations. In the coming chapters, you will see the variants of blockchains that result from varying parameters of consensus, storage, cryptography types, and so forth.

How Does a Blockchain Work?

Now that we have learned what blockchains are, let us examine how they work for you in the big picture.

Even in today's digital age, a lot of corporations struggle to connect stakeholders and processes across different departments and geographies. Hence, there is an urge to link these isolated processes and have a single source of truth. For example, the accounts department might have its own system for calculating the expenses of each branch location, which might not always resonate with the expenses reported by the administration department. However, there are governance processes and checks and balances in place to take care of this problem, but it entails a lot of manual effort and audits. If the same system were to be on a blockchain, all the stakeholders would be getting the same value of branch expenses. This would happen because the consensus policies ensure the credibility of any data added by the users. From a small time business to a multinational organization, a process if put on blockchain would showcase the online presence of all data generated in a process. The awareness of this entire network is the key to optimizing and leveraging the process flows better, thereby enabling trust. If you understand your network and ecosystem, figuring out the sweet spot of business operations is a cake walk. For instance, figuring out supply and demand ensures low inventory costs and low out-of-stock costs. Similarly, digitally understanding your network opens up a whole new understanding of trade, in several ways pro-actively.

In a multi-tier network architecture, in situations where 10,000 subscribers are hitting the servers at once, the demand is channeled and distributed into different logical queues to serve back information. In the case of a single-server client network, this situation would have required scaling the server to accommodate such a user base.

With a peer-to-peer network, not only is the load distributed throughout the chain, but also the security is decentralized throughout. The validation is not just for one to decide or approve, but for the network majority to decide.

Next, we cover blockchains in different ecosystems.

As an Individual

Imagine being a business owner with a few clients who don't pay on time. Smart contracts trigger automatically to enforce pre-agreed conditions. So, if you locked your clients into a smart contract that has a clause that charges 2 percent interest for every month of delay, the invoice's value gets updated on the ledger upon every delay. The value of the amount owed by the client increases. Likewise, the client is empowered to expect timely delivery on such a smart contract. If the delivery is not met, the client can have a pre-defined program that penalizes the business owner 2 percent for the delayed month. This smart contract is undeniable due to the chain of validators ensuring its execution and enforcement.

In an Office Department

Imagine you head a team of 25 people in the Quality Check of Assembly for an Engineering Product. This department works on the functional processes such as:

1. Visual check of Assembly

2. Aggregation of defective images of the assembly

3. Annotations of the Defects in the image & identification of the type of defect

4. Diagnosis for the defect

5. Identification of the stakeholder for the recommended diagnostic

6. Getting it fixed

7. Updating Assembly with fix

8. Final check to close case

As the head of the department, you ensure the assembly of the Engineering Product goes through perfectly with no defects. Each functional process mentioned is handled by different stakeholder in your department. Now traditionally, this record of who does what is known to you & can be stored in a standard ERP.

Consider a scenario where a major fault was detected by your customer leading to heavy losses & the insurer is investigating over the point of failure.

Based on the ERP, record, the last quality check was approved by you based on the working documents produced by your team. This ERP may be tampered thereby endangering credibility of information.

Hence the Blockchain here stores the trace of work in a manner that no data can be tampered, thereby maintaining credibility of information & security.

In a Company Across Branches

Imagine a company with branches across the country and people scattered all over. The strategy head has to wait for reports to be aggregated from all zonal managers. All zonal managers have to reach out to regional heads. All regional heads have to extract data from local offices. This set of actions is every large-scale company's nightmare. Sure, there are SAPs, ERPs, and several types of software for it. But how many times have these data points been tampered with, tweaked, and modified on their way to the top? It is highly questionable.

In a Group of Companies

Consider a Fortune 500 group of companies that are in almost 20 different industry sectors, with products that may work for their very own employees. The awareness of the companies in the group is barely transparent. Whatever is aggregated in newsletters, company events, and the website is purely based on brand perception and not on the true value worth.

Now, imagine this to be a hybrid network of private and public blockchains within the company group.

The public blockchain can have metadata that speaks about each of these companies' structures, leadership, and products. The private blockchain may have confidential numbers for salaries, targets, and so on.

People always question why a blockchain is required for such purposes. The same information could be found on a website or a Power Point presentation. The problem with these forms is that the website becomes a vulnerable target for hackers if it is not meant to be in the public domain, but just on the private ledger that is open to employees. A presentation deck may be copied, downloaded, and sent to the wrong people offline without a trace. So, these mediums fail, and blockchains are a better option. The private blockchains could be restricted to senior management so they can make a fully informed decision with all sources shown on the ledger.

In a Group of Inter-country Trades

By studying the macroeconomics of world trade, we can all understand the factors that cause variations in our currencies. The value of world trade is one of the factors. Demand and supply year by year vary from product to product, service to service. The market shifts often, and so economies are altered by market corrections, loan policies, government grants, and so forth. A lot of these changes are policy driven, with attempts to increase predictability. However, it always remains a questionable affair as to whether it works as planned or falls apart due to the many variables involved. Getting data correct has always been a need, and digitizing data really started in the last decade. Meanwhile, digitizing credible *true* sources of data has begun, with blockchains ensuring the digitizing process encapsulates structured, secure, credible data.

Across the Globe

With increased connectivity, having access to every part of the globe directly without intermediaries opens up exciting avenues of opportunity. Credible education, high-quality food, energy distributions, good jobs, and so forth all become more accessible (see Figure 1-10).

The Global Trade Chain

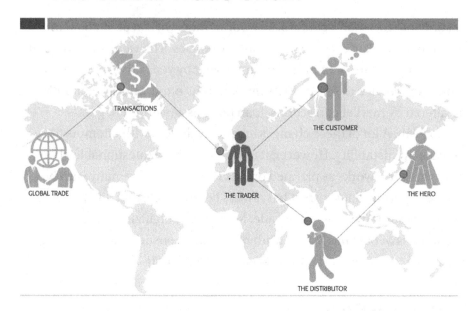

Figure 1-10. *The global trade chain*

With all these ecosystems now restructured into a credible infrastructure, we see that how we deal with one another will change greatly, with our processes being digitized and our data being more structured than ever.

It changes organizational design. It changes world trade. It changes how we assign value. It gives a chance for fair trade and fair valuation of effort if rightly captured within blockchains. It reforms policies into mutually agreeable contracts. It eliminates the room for the manipulation of data that was once committed to in a transaction.

Consensus Algorithms

From Stone Age man to an evolved society, large-scale movements have been driven when people believe in them. That belief drove a lot of societal vision. This very belief is digitized into consensus algorithms in blockchains. These consensus algorithms are executed when there is agreement on a certain principle. This forms the core of blockchains in all types of networks. Peers in the network, when in consensus, allow transaction activity through the blockchain network. The forms of consensus may vary based on the application and the level of criticality.

The forms of consensus are based on the required methods of agreement that usually occur in an offline scenario. For example, when a community decides that a certain degree is required for a profession, it basically unknowingly validates this offline agreement. For a real-life example, one may consider the role of an architect. The people who form the civilization create a consensus of trust that the person with the architecture degree can handle the structural designs of buildings.

Now that we have understood a real life consensus scenario, Blockchain provides the infrastructure to digitize this very mutual agreement on a software connected to all stakeholders participating in the process of making a decision.

Therefore, consensus algorithms form the most crucial part of blockchains when transactions and contracts are actualized on a chain.

Think of the thought leadership that is evident in successfully liberated democracies. The drivers of such leadership are the people and their belief networks. The digital version of this is the consensus algorithm. In the world of blockchains, various blockchains follow various forms of consensus based on the structure of their network, the data on the chain, and the types of transaction activity.

One such famous consensus algorithm, Proof of Work, is utilized by Bitcoin and Ethereum. Several other mechanisms follow, such as the following:

- Proof of Work

    The peers that wish to engage in a transaction on the chain are required to solve a complex problem, spending time and energy to solve it and proving their interest to engage. The value of the spend is the processing time.

- Proof of Stake

  The voting mechanism here for block producers to
  pass data on the chain requires the agreement of the
  stakeholder majority based on the condition of the
  stake (wealth, age, seniority, etc.).

- Delegated Proof of Stake

  An implementation of technology-based
  democracy, using voting and election processes
  to protect the blockchain from centralization and
  malicious usage. Here, instead of the stakeholder,
  the voting rights are delegated at random or are
  based on delegation so as to decentralize power.

- Proof of Weight

  The agreement on the chain is dependent on the
  amount of tokens held by a peer and the probability
  of finding the next block reward.

- Proof of Elapsed Time

  This is used in private chains when adding peers
  to the network. The agreement is reached over the
  time elapsed to validate new peers' onboarding
  based on dynamic snooze times.

- Proof of Authority

  Consensus agreement over any data or transaction
  happens only by the validators who are assigned
  the authority to validate. This may be coupled with
  Federated Byzantine Agreement.

However, as an early adopter of blockchains, one must understand that the preceding items are just mechanisms that have been used to form consensus. One can develop one's own principle or mechanism or merge multiple methods to reach consensus in one's networks as desired. Note that the consensus algorithms are set and pre-defined during the setup of the blockchains for any network. Updating with a new form may require the consensus of the network.

With the choice of the blockchain framework made, the consensus comes along. For example, Ethereum initially worked based on the Proof of Work mechanism, where the value on the chain is generated by mining, and the transaction utility also utilizes this value. Therefore, the consensus was reached purely based on the proof of work done on the chain. Now, Ethereum is working based on the adoption of Proof of Stake, where the value of the network movement is independent of mining or any such efforts but proportional to the stake the peers have in the network. The needs and demands of the network form the choice of consensus.

A person skeptical of accepting this common agreement principle in the form of consensus algorithms may question whether it is really programmed for true consensus. They may question whether there are any loopholes in such consensus algorithms on blockchains where crucial trade activities could be conducted. This point of worry is solved with the open source nature of these blockchains, where the source code is laid open for critical review. Therefore, all parties agreeing on the chain are assured of the genuineness of the algorithm.

Such conflicts are usually a concern when Enterprise businesses engage on blockchains that have a common form of mutually accepted consensus. The open source nature of such frameworks plays a crucial part. Azure's Blockchain Workbench ensures the routing connectors to such blockchain frameworks have flawless integrations and infrastructural connectivity.

Now that we understand the business perspective surrounding consensus, we will break down the technical needs of consensus for blockchains. For developers who code for inter-business or inter-departmental operations, there are zillions of cases that must be met. In a peer-to-peer network, where every peer's environment may differ from the others, executing a truly decentralized activity on a blockchain may impact a lot of different workflows. Thus, such a network requires a common principle by which to achieve decentralization in decision-making and transaction activities. Therefore, the need for consensus. Consider race condition situations, or the million concurrent user requests that need to be serviced—which situation must be given priority is thereby decided and governed via the principle defined in the consensus algorithm.

This book examines different variants of consensus while discussing various use cases. Remember the choice of consensus must be user/data/transaction-centric so as to emulate societal agreements in a more tangible form.

Azure and Blockchains

With the increase of technology awareness, and its widespread impact across industries, domains, sectors, groups of people, markets, and ecosystems, the need for better processes is also increasing. Focusing on a vision of being change-makers, companies attempt to streamline operations with technology to enhance work quality. Traditional industries that have existed for decades have tons of data and people all across the globe who are actively running processes in widely distributed departments, locations, and so forth. Given the competitiveness of the market, various employee expectations, consumer transparency, and the speed of decision-making, the adoption of blockchains to form a truly decentralized ecosystem is inevitable. Several companies already have enterprise software that collates data. But to get the very people interacting with the software to feed in credible timely data is a huge deal, especially in companies that have offices across countries. This is exactly where Azure extends its connectivity and enterprise suite of integrations with blockchains as shown in Figure 1-11.

So, before we dive further into this book, let's account for the transitions that may be required to ensure a decentralized network using blockchains.

Authorizations of Users on a Chain

Enterprises use Active Directory by Azure, which ensures the authentication and security of employee logins, customer logins, and so on. With Azure Blockchain Workbench, integration with the Azure Active Directory is seamless. Identity management is sorted with minimal effort. This allows businesses to handle authorization, access control, and user roles. When two businesses intend to engage with each other, their respective AD management can be linked without compromising decentralization.

Once the Azure AD users are registered, the rightful application under Azure Workbench can be linked, thereby mapping the existing user identities from a centralized system to decentralized blockchain identities. User management is entirely anonymized on the chain wherever required with Azure's AD mapping.

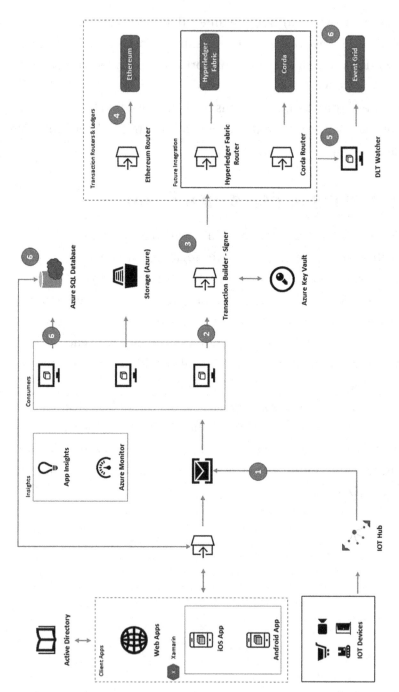

Figure 1-11. An example of blockchain deployment on Azure

Metadata of Existing Information

When multiple businesses engage with the blockchain, each comes with its own set of crucial metadata. This data is to be maintained privately for internal operations, and parts of it may be crucial for on-chain inter-operational activities between businesses. Workbench supports the off-loading of chain data to SQL servers for analysis and vice versa to maintain flexibility and privacy. Further, it enables the integration of blockchains with other Azure services via the Azure Blockchain Workbench for event triggers, external APIs, IoT hubs, and so on, with the flexibility of programming in Java, .NET, and Python through the open API integrations provided by Workbench.

Process Challenges That Require Blockchains

Before integrating Azure components with the blockchain, designing the workflow, process flow, and data flow is crucial. The key management, off-chain service integrations, and logic apps can all be connected in various forms. Organizational design and inter-organizational design have to be mutually accepted or use an existing framework that is agreeable to all parties.

Business Applications and Presentation Tools

Workbench provides a huge set of integrations with logic apps and data monitors—such as network monitors, DLT watchers, and so on—that send alerts in the case of any event triggers like down times, bottlenecks, etc. Logs are maintained for every state of movement. Elements such as Power BI and analytic tools provision better forms of visualization of the ongoing activities.

This makes it a complete suite of infrastructure tools for anyone who wishes to decentralize. As we will see with several social media community managers empowered to run their groups online or over chats, the Azure Blockchain Workbench allows users to set up a peer-to-peer network with the array of supporting tools showcased.

CHAPTER 2

Decoding a Real-Life Blockchain

This chapter sets the stage to unfold various elements of blockchains throughout the book.

Let these flash cards (in Figure 2-1) circulate around in your head, and we will see how real-world applications bind them to a successful blockchain implementation.

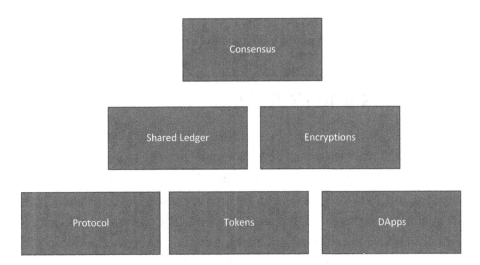

Figure 2-1. *Flash cards for aspects of blockchains*

© Shilpa Karkeraa 2020
S. Karkeraa, *Unlocking Blockchain on Azure*,
https://doi.org/10.1007/978-1-4842-5043-3_2

These flash cards are arranged top to bottom in the sequence in which they are to be considered when building a blockchain.

For this chapter, the real-life blockchain platform making literal waves across the ocean is **BBChain—Blackbox on Blockchains**, which brings a very interesting use case for blockchains from which we can learn. We will decode each element of the blockchain and see how it is embedded into the platform, changing the way maritime data moves across the globe. Highlights of this chapter are as follows:

- Purpose and principle behind the blockchain—consensus and protocols

- Transforming a centralized platform into a decentralized blockchain—shared ledgers

- Securing data throughout the chain—encryption

- Valuing the chain and its utility to stakeholders—tokens

- The end picture—decentralized applications (DApps)

- Setting up blockchain environments on Azure

Consensus and Protocols

Every decade, several ships on the ocean and aircraft in the expanse of the sky disappear. Lives are lost, and no traces are left to be found.

These lives count, and so does the data related to these accidents. Therefore, BBChain attempts to handle the voyage data recorder (VDR) data over blockchains through decentralization. The conventional black boxes or VDRs on the ships record all the goings on onboard the ship. However, it sinks with the lost ship, nowhere to be found in some cases.

While several technologies came and went over the decades, the latest era of technologists formulated to store VDR data on the cloud. VDR providers would sync the box data to a centralized cloud server, to which the black box would transmit at various time intervals.

By revolutionizing the black box with BBChain's protocol that uses blockchains, we will learn how consensus plays a very important role in enhancing the credibility of the black box (Figure 2-2).

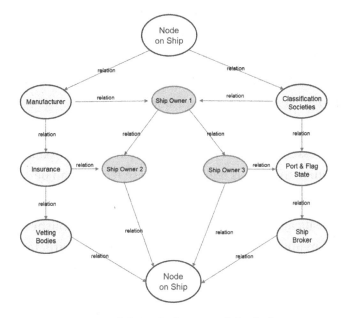

Figure 2-2. *Illustration of the BBChain public ledger*

As seen in Figure 2-2, the main stakeholders involved in the shipping trade include the following:

- Blackbox on Blockchain as Node (IoT device): This device enters all on-ship measurements, sensory data, and travel data in real-time to the blockchain node syncing with the entire network.

- Ship Owners: These users are able to transparently see the real-time situation of the ship and can keep tabs.

- Manufacturer: Ship manufacturers maintain service contracts for the ship for years. Being on the chain lets them be in the loop of the nautical miles traveled and required maintenance done.

- Insurance Companies: During audits, insurance companies require the complete audit trail of records of the state of the ship throughout its history. Connecting on-chain enables immutable records.

- Ship Brokers: On-chain history provides credibility for ship brokers to recommend ships.

- Port and Flag State: Port state is the location where the vessel/ship enters the water, whereas the flag state is where the ship is registered. These records can be onboarded credibly by these entities on the chain.

- Classification Societies: Organization that establishes and maintains technical standards for the construction and operation of ships and offshore structures

- Vetting Bodies: These organizations evaluate the ship's structural integrity and performance, and perform audits and quality checks to form a standardized grading system.

The chain of all these stakeholders of the maritime industry forms the nodes of the blockchain for the public ledger. For any change made to this public ledger, all stakeholders must be in consensus given the pre-defined protocol of that blockchain. Currently, the interaction of these stakeholders is entirely paper based—or is transitioning to being cloud based with digital documents.

Before we dive into the form of consensus used by BBChain, let us review what consensus means in simple terms:

Consensus—A generally accepted opinion or decision among a group of people

—Cambridge Dictionary

The core of any blockchain lies in its consensus. On a blockchain, a group of nodes (servers/peer instances representing users) participating in the chain reaches an agreement on a base principle that is coded into a set of rules for every single piece of data or state across the network. This is achieved through a distributed process across all nodes. Every blockchain may or may not be governed by different consensus mechanisms.

For example, Bitcoin and Ethereum work on the proof of work consensus mechanism. Every time a block equation is solved (work), tokens are awarded to the individuals validating the transaction.

Further, Ethereum is pursuing a shift to the proof of stake consensus mechanism, where, instead of work, the stake (ownership value) takes precedence in forming an agreement.

Here's a view of different types of consensus governing various blockchains.

Blockchain Name	Consensus Mechanism	Description
Bitshares	Delegated Proof of Stake	Mechanism where nodes can delegate the responsibility of having a stake to another node to validate a transaction
NEM	Proof of Importance	Important nodes have high transactional control

(*continued*)

Blockchain Name	Consensus Mechanism	Description
Stellar	Federated Byzantine Agreement	Quorum slices chosen at random form intersections to validate a transaction on behalf of all nodes
Corda	Consensus over State Validity Uniqueness	Nodes reach certainty based on the validity of the contract over input and output states as well as the uniqueness of the output, such that the input was never consumed before
EOS	Byzantine Fault Tolerance—Delegated Proof of Stake	Selection of block producers through a continuous approval voting system that runs with a fault-tolerant mechanism

The recent rise in popularity of this technology and the large flow of funds toward it are mainly due to the consensus-regulated nature of such platforms. The quantification of effort, value, and processes has increased tenfold in this era that has a growing digital footprint.

Thus, as a software architect, how do we decide on the suitability of a principle for a blockchain platform?

1. Start with understanding the application

2. Break down and understand the existing digital form of the application at hand.

3. Identify the limitations of the current setup that one is aiming to solve.

4. Question which aspect of the application requires decentralization, tokenization, or encryption.

5. Segment the audience for the application—random open users or restricted invite-only users?

6. Analyze the audience dynamics.

With BBChain, the answers to the preceding questions were as follows:

1. A platform for voyage data to be shared across stakeholders

2. Existing solutions are on ship or on centralized cloud servers

3. Data can be manipulated or lost, leading to conspiracies over lost ships and aircraft in existing solutions

4. Data on a shared decentralized ledger, with the value of the data quantified with tokens and secured channels of operations, such that data cannot be manipulated or modified without the agreement of the stakeholders involved

5. Audiences of the maritime industry, such as ship owners, port owners, manufacturers, port and flag states, insurance companies, and private users

6. The users may be the stakeholders of the public ledger that enlists the data of the ship voyages, vessel names, type of data, locations, ports, and routes. Further users like insurers may want to know more than the information on the shared public ledger. Thus, one must require that the insurer subscribes to private data on the private ledger.

Thus, the following configuration of a hybrid network that has a combination of public and private ledgers would work (Figure 2-3):

- Public Ledger: A chain of nodes where data is shared publicly with all nodes, and every transaction is validated publicly across the chain via a commonly agreed upon consensus of that chain. Anyone can openly invite new members to such a chain and add blocks transparently.

- Private Ledger: A chain of selective nodes that exclusively have access to private data and selective validating rights to form consensus internally with a permissioned set of capacities.

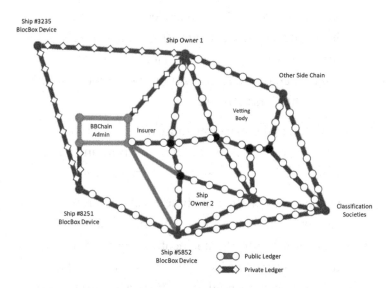

Figure 2-3. *Visual representation of a hybrid network of various stakeholders*

The BBChain protocol provides a way to reach consensus for the maritime peer-to-peer network of stakeholders for voyage data. The chain is a hybrid blockchain of private chains involving the BBChain node, ship owner, and the IoT devices on the ship, and a public chain that includes all maritime stakeholders, as shown in Figure 2-3. Private chains can be formed on the fly when there are private transactions on the chain. Several such private chains are called side chains and form out of public chains.

Consensus in this protocol can only be reached with a blend of the following:

- Federated Byzantine Agreement

- Proof of stake

- Proof of importance

The foundation of the protocol uses the Federated Byzantine Agreement on the public ledger, which includes all peers of the maritime industry, consisting of manufacturers, port and flag states, ship owners, and other stakeholders. Hence, let's deep dive into the protocol and understand it better, using Figure 2-3.

Federated Byzantine Agreement

As shown in Figure 2-3, the public ledger in yellow connects everyone in the chain. The data distribution for public data is entirely contained on this ledger configuration. This consensus encompasses the principles of FBA (Federated Byzantine Agreement, explained later in this book), with its fault-tolerant capabilities. So, all the ship voyage data that are publicly open to all stakeholders, such as ship routes, locations, and voyage schedules, are openly shared across the ledger. Any stakeholder interested in knowing more about any voyage can then initiate the contract request to join the private ledger to know more about that ship voyage.

Figure 2-4 shows the append-only feature of BBChain, which shows every state of data on the blockchain ledger. Every transaction on the public chain is witnessed by all stakeholders.

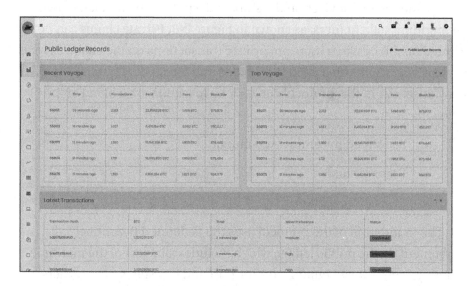

Figure 2-4. *Public ledger records*

Similarly transparency over Voyage Statuses (Figure 2-5), type of purchases of voyage data & other actions are witnessed & validated by Public Chain Nodes.

Figure 2-5. *Public ledger records—where legit data can be purchased transparently*

The platform allows one to purchase voyage data transparently and benefits the rightful stakeholders, including the ship owner and data owner.

You can think of this as a listing of air ticket options on travel websites.

Now, the question here is, if that's what a public ledger on a blockchain is, then why not just have the old-school website listings on the internet that are already there?

Many listings, such as Monster Jobs, Expedia, and, for that matter, Amazon, are all out there, providing a great amount of information publicly.

However, many times, the data on such platforms is purely controlled by only the companies running them. Thus, the democracy of real users is entirely ignored in such cases. Every time a Terms and Conditions pop-up appears, many online users are forced to sign it and use the centralized platform. Many times, fraudulent activities that are difficult to trace for the centralized platforms themselves cause several inconveniences, such as fake jobs, false offers, or improper products. The access control to manipulate the displayed data on centralized platforms is far more liberal as it does not need all validators to validate many times. Also, if no proper notification system is designed on such centralized platforms, users may not even know the change, thereby making the data highly mutable and less reliable.

That's where the blockchain over a public ledger brings full transparency to all its users to trace every data addition or transaction, knowing the source of such additions and approving allowing the data to pass in the first place.

However, let's not mistake transparency for having no privacy. That's another strong aspect of blockchain that involves the encryption of data that's distributed across the ledger (explained in the coming subsections).

 Trivia   Name three applications that can be decentralized onto a public ledger.

Proof of Stake

The BBChain on a ship transmits data to the ledger network. However, not all of it is publicly available due to the data's sensitivity and the ownership of the data. Thus, such data is an asset to the ship owner, who is a high-level stakeholder. They can decide to extend their data to the stakeholders they wish to share it with. For example, the ship owner needs to claim insurance for the ship. Here, the ship owner, who has a high stake in the data, can decide to create an internal private ledger in the form a side chain (highlighted in aqua blue in Figure 2-3).

🧠 Challenge   Similarly, think how your stock exchange would work over a blockchain.

- Enlist which datapoints go onto the public ledger and private ledger.

- Identify all stakeholders crucial to using this blockchain.

- Identify the operations required on-chain and off-chain.

- Enlist the on-chain operations and define the mandatory principles.

- Draw out the structure, operations, and stakeholders, as in Figures 2-3, 2-4, and 2-5.

BBChain's side chain will share private information across the contracted stakeholders. The contract will be a digital contract that programmatically allows users to agree on certain points, such as the quantity of data, type, price of subscription, and expiry. This internal chain works on proof of stake, as only the ones who have significant stakes can access the chain, contribute data, and view the data and transactions. At the start, the ship owner will have the maximum stake for their ship's data, for obvious reasons, which will be distributed based on the subscriptions through the initial contract to other stakeholders. The ship owner—the block producer—delegates certain stakes to other producers when they contribute in the private chain so they become subscribers that receive private data (such as insurance reports, audits, etc.).

Proof of Importance

After the first two configurations are set up, the proof of importance method is used for the transfer of data across the chain and the priority access, which is based on the cumulative value of transactions on the ledger for that node. This helps to handle high-demand traffic scenarios in the event of interest from several stakeholders at the same time. The nodes may gain importance, or the transaction may gain importance based on the amount of tokens, size of data, and traction of data.

With the blend of these three mechanisms, we formed the BBChain Protocol.

Challenge   Design a consensus mechanism for the following applications:

1. Housing Society activities, such as electing members, approval of NOCs (No Objection Certificates), etc.

2. Food raw materials ledger with quality control

Shared Ledgers

The traditional centralized cloud-based servers from the last era are everywhere, be it e-commerce platforms or media channels or the television industry. The ads we see and the programs that are hosted have a more centralized, commercial approach.

🧠 Trivia   Identify the highly centralized platforms that show dominance on large markets:

- Is highly mutable (can be manipulated by anyone—hackers, jammers, etc.)

- Can be lost due to faults, write failures, and server downtimes

- Vulnerable to data leaks and privacy

- Low access control and is in control of the solution provider

---

This has led to several conspiracies about lost ships and aircraft.

The concept of BBChain revamps the old-school storage and hosting options with new-age decentralized transparent shared ledgers. The append-only data on the ledgers can be truly trusted as the sole source of truth, be secured, and have a direct connection and reliability with the correct stakeholders.

Let's come back to the same question: Why blockchain? Why decentralize to a shared ledger?

In the olden days, when democracy wasn't fully matured, the dominance of some influential individuals or companies was more prevalent. From getting a telephone line to applying for a visa, things were entirely dependent on centralized authorities. As society progressed, democracy's structure improved among the individuals, and a larger group of people was involved in decision-making, laws and rights, and the way we work.

This era of millennials wouldn't entirely be aware of the pain it took to access certain opportunities before the internet. Now that we are in this digital age where the internet is a common commodity, structuring the software applications we use is important. For example, on a social media platform, where one uploads a photo and chooses to delete it, the data authority of the photo is entirely lost by the individual when he uploads it to this centralized platform (this might get changed with the GDPR Regulations; however, enforcement and checks may be manual). So, with the comparison of the age when we didn't have democracy with the current era, blockchain brings that opportunity to give every identity a voice to structure, vote, and contribute to this digital era. In technical terms, every device becomes an access control touchpoint, every computer becomes a storage point, every user exercises voting rights, and every policy that can be automated across the shared ledger brings in transparency, data decentralization, privacy, security, immutability, and validity of every transaction and action on such platforms. This is what this book envisions educating all its readers about.

Examples of blockchains—i.e., shared ledgers—that are bringing about social impact are as follows:

- UN World Food Programme (WFP) started a program called Building Blocks in 2016, which uses the Ethereum blockchain to make "WFP's growing cash-based transfer operations faster, cheaper, and more secure," according to the project's website. This was piloted to track assistance to Syrian refugees.

- Invested in by the UNICEF Innovations Fund, the blockchain platform Amply and IXO provide transparency for funding transactions for charities helping with South African education.

- The Brooklyn Microgrid is changing the way we choose our electricity source, such as solar yielded at private homes, transmissioned energy, etc., driving an economy that is truly decentralized for production and consumption with direct demand and supply connectivity through a shared ledger.

- M-Vision is a decentralized incubator that runs on blockchains and quantifies remote research efforts and brings them closer to commercialization through the ledger network of researchers, professionals, and industrialists.

Coming back to BBChain, we shared public data, showcased in Figures 2-4 and 2-5, on the shared ledger by using the principles of BigChainDB and Cassandra to store data in a distributed manner.

Here is a storage simulation of financial data in a centralized platform versus decentralization:

- Centralized/Normal Platform:

  ```
  X = "Confidential Info: 1 Million USD
  Transferred to Dr. John Doe"
  ```

  – Stored as an encrypted record in a database stored on a single server

- Decentralized Platform/Blockchain:

  ```
  Y = Encrypt (X), break X into pieces and store
  in N number of nodes on the ledger
  ```

  – Making it difficult for any fraudulent user or network jammer to decrypt and retrieve X, as first the hacker would require the complete form of the encrypted sentence and then the decryption key, which also may be distributed across the chain.

BBChain distributes and locks data securely on-chain over the shared ledger.

💭 **Challenge**   From the preceding information, identify which aspect of dominance of an online platform can be restructured on a distributed ledger.

For example, in trade finance, financial institutions are the dominant authorities that can issue the letters of credit and bank guarantees for large-scale import-export activities. The dominance aspect here is for the issuance, which is democratized with the rules and checks defined by the authorities. However, this issuance can have human biases and influences at times, causing defaulters. This aspect of trust and authority when automated over a smart contract on a shared ledger brings a better chance of avoiding trade defaults. So, this challenge asks the readers to identify which part of dominance one wishes to reprogram, and this book will help you construct and program the same.

Encryption

When we log in to a bank portal or a Social Security system, the sense of security and trust is perceived, whereas on open platforms for photo sharing and social media, data is a lot more open than one's bank account details.

💭 **Trivia**   Spot the top three differences in perceived security between your social media accounts and your digital bank accounts.

Now, where does this link to the aspects of blockchain where we call it transparent, shared, and secure? There are several blockchain platforms for various purposes, like there are several existing online applications for social media as well as financial transactions. The underlying concept that embeds trust on a blockchain is the end-to-end encryption of the data such that the immutable data can only be decrypted when the consensus is formed among the participating nodes. Here, we use Shamir's secret sharing algorithm for distributed split-key management. Different blockchain platforms can engage different mechanisms of key management depending on the criticality of the data. Using split-key management on the distributed ledger makes it difficult for a hacker to hack externally, unless a 51% mining attack (where major nodes/users are fraudulent ones) occurs among the chain stakeholders.

The very famous and the oldest Blockchain Cryptocurrency Bitcoin is a digital currency known as electronic cash where transactions were made across the network nodes cryptographically with SHA256. Each block contains a SHA256 cryptographic hash of the previous block thus linking it to the previous block and giving the blockchain its name. To be accepted by the rest of the network, a new block must contain the Proof of Work. Miners rely on computing the "SHA256 Hash Function" for a lot of inputs until they find the nonce for a given block before adding it to the blockchain.

In Figure 2-4, we saw that the encryption and chunking of the data across the ledger makes it difficult for hackers or external users to retrieve any relevant information.

Let's come back to the topic of social media, where we enjoy social attention from our network of friends and families upon sharing posts, photos, and personal views. When such data is directly uploaded to a server, the network and the server are susceptible to attacks or being accessed by any other unauthorized user knowingly or unknowingly. This can cause data leaks to land in the wrong hands at times.

Now, imagine the scenario of using blockchains for social media. The functionalities would be the same. But how data is stored and managed is different. On a blockchain, the user's node encrypts the data and uploads it to the ledger. Based on the consensus mechanism of that chain, data is tokenized and distributed among stakeholders with whom the user wishes to share. For any node or user to read this data, it must decrypt the entire sequence of distributed data stored across several nodes, making it highly secure and requiring more computations to crack.

There are various techniques of encryption used in distributed ledgers. One can decide based on the application and type of blockchain.

BBChain uses ED25519 for end-to-end encryption, especially for the private ledger side chains where more confidential data is shared. In a hybrid network such as BBChain, where users are on both private and public ledgers, key-sharing mechanisms are used to encrypt and decrypt data that is shared on the blockchain.

Several cryptographic mechanisms, such as the SHA 2 Family, Shamir's Secret Sharing, and EdDSA techniques, are widely used in blockchains. Imagine a user who is acquainted with setting up passwords—how will we enable them to encrypt their data securely on a blockchain? One way could be by using a pre-defined set of encryption rules on the blockchain or giving them the capability to choose their set of encryption techniques. In technical terms, the user on a blockchain may be a node/server dispatching data (to add a block). Thus, the encryption is set on this server where the data is originating through his private key. On-chain users may retrieve data using the public key and further decrypt it using the private key. Such combinations of encryption options are provided by the mechanisms mentioned here.

 Challenge   Prepare three encryption packages that may be utilized on your social media data such as photographs, posts, and location.

Tokens

Across centuries, nations, tribes, and humans in general have been attempting to quantify efforts to trade, be it the age-old barter systems or the modern era of financial transactions. The right quantification of time, space, and economies has been volatile throughout.

Bitcoin utilizes the proof of work method, which helps to quantify the value of the token. The computing power to make one transaction across all nodes translates to the value of the Bitcoin by solving the equation. Thus, transacting in this digital currency has enabled trade over such cryptocurrencies.

A cryptocurrency is a digital or virtual currency that uses cryptography for security.

—Investopedia

Several blockchains have successfully quantified the value of the tokens through their ability to scale, operate, and impact in the form of security tokens or utility tokens.

Security tokens are usually the famously listed ICOs, or cryptocurrencies, that receive investments through stakeholders that value the concept and operations of the decentralized blockchain platform.

Utility tokens are the ones that are valued purely for their usage. The usage is quantified with the mechanism of the blockchain, like the value generated by proof of work, as explained earlier.

With BBChain, the utility of the tokens generates the security value. The users of the chain transact with using this utility token on BBChain, to view, subscribe, and buy maritime ship data from other users.

Now the question is, in the world of existing economies of different nations, how does one trust the so-called true value of the chain?

The value of the chain is decided based on the pre-designed nature of the chain, which is based on the consensus and its protocol.

Let's see how BBChain does it.

BBChain Protocol encapsulates a blend of three consensus mechanisms; i.e., Federated Byzantine Agreement (FBA), proof of stake (POS), and proof of importance (POI). The public ledger is governed with FBA. The private ledger is regulated by the POS. POI governs universally across both public and private chains.

Consider N nodes on the public ledger as $n1$, $n2$, $n3$, $n4$ ... nN. The movements on the blockchain are drawn with the validations from the quorum intersections for the public data for transactions and decisions, thus using the principle of FBA to form consensus on public ledger activities.

Under the BBChain Protocol, data producers gain stakes in a private chain with the BBChain Genesis Node. Further, these data producers (ship owners, port owners, manufacturers) may subcontract their stakes to other users in this private side chain. Based on the smart contract, stakes are redistributed. While exchanging stakes, the value of the importance of every node and state is recalculated in the private as well as the public chain on the basis of the following:

1. Stake value of the nodes at a given time in private ledgers

2. Comparative/relative value of stake across all private ledgers

3. All-time stake average throughout the year

4. Threshold calculation of the vesting amount to become a stake owner

5. Threshold calculation for a stake owner to initiate the side ledger

6. Threshold calculations for anyone to join a side ledger

7. Value of block and number of blocks

8. Age of the block and size of group of blocks

9. State of block (data traction and freshness)

10. Total value of tokens in a chain and the minimum vested value on a node

Data Flow Sequencing

Since the prime element that moves across BBChain is the maritime data, let us understand the flow of data & the impacting factors based on the consensus algorithms & the transactions on chain as per the following sequence:

1. On prioritizing transactions, states, and data across the chain, the value of importance is calculated on the preceding factors and will have calculated thresholds for every node to be able to perform some activities.

2. This calculation takes precedence for data rendering mainly when we have high concurrency and data congestion in a limited node and hardware/network bandwidth scenario.

3. Other actions, such as creating a side ledger, distributing data for subscriptions, and generating data requests for internal (highly private data), require the nodes to cross a certain value of importance to join the consensus (like joining a side ledger).

4. Nodes with data that are obsolete (decided by the factor of age of block, e.g., > 5 years, or highly redundant to no traction for a large set of data blocks) can be removed from the chain as a rule under the protocol, with an option to centralize and store.

5. Nodes can raise a request from the public ledger to access that data, and high-importance nodes can perform consensus using the FBA mechanism to allow/validate the request.

Decentralized Applications

After understanding all the building blocks of the blockchain, we saw how every fundamental element weaves into an application to form the decentralized ledger to a completely running blockchain. This does not form just a software but also a very powerful ecosystem that can drive economies of this digital age.

Every blockchain signifies a strong aspect of quantification and consensus. There have been several existing distributed databases, ledgers, processes, and systems, so what makes blockchains so crucial and different is the right time, ecosystem, and the ability to monetize the true value system behind the blockchain.

Coming back to BBChain, which brings a highly credible data source to its stakeholders from maritime voyages, the standards set for its value are simply generated by the parameters mentioned in the previous section.

Questions that formulate around such a decentralized application are as follows:

- What is the core digital asset of your chain?

- What are the key stakeholders doing with the digital asset?

- How does one maintain the security of the digital asset?

- How are the contracts and consensus maintained to honor the digital transaction for the asset?

- Which technologies fall in line with the requirements of the blockchain application?

- Is scalability required? How is scalability maintained?

Answers for BBChain are as follows, respectively:

- Voyage data is the key digital asset.

- Stakeholders such as block producers (ship owners, port owners) generate data, whereas insurers and shipping authorities subscribe/buy such data. Data as blocks are transferred in various side chains and on the public ledger.

- As the complete encrypted digital asset (by the public key) is broken down and distributed with a fault-tolerant consensus among different nodes, upon the rightful consensus, the location of the data packet is revealed to the correct stakeholder. On accumulating all the data packets in the right sequence, the decryption will be valid with the use of the private key by the correct stakeholder.

- The rightful stakeholder has a contract in place with the block producer/buyer. On creation of the contract, the public key and the private key are generated based on the expiry of the contract. The key expires along with the contract. The consensus among the private ledger is governed by the proof of stake. This is validated by all the stakeholders of that side chain who shared the distributed data on their servers in encrypted form.

- The architecture supports the technologies required to suit the conditions of the chain (Figure 2-6).

63

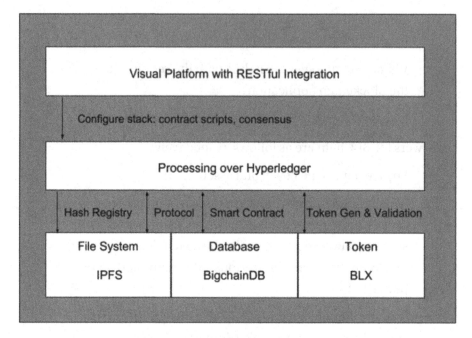

Figure 2-6. *Architecture for BBChain components*

- As the voyage data of a ship records every moment of the voyage, scalability is required on the ledger. This is managed by the storage mechanisms provided by BigChainDB and IPFS.

Challenge   Provide your version of answers to the preceding questions as if you were to export goods and transact over a blockchain. Jot down thoughts and compare notes with the use case provided in the upcoming chapters.

Setting Blockchain Environments

By now, we have covered all fundamentals of blockchains, in theory. Now, let's head to the practical implementation to set up a blockchain infrastructure.

For this section, we will deploy a blockchain on the Azure Blockchain Workbench. Think of this as a package suite of infrastructural elements that contribute to building a blockchain, like IKEA assembly instructions for making a bed or a wardrobe. Azure makes the deployment a lot more accelerated, as the infrastructure elements are taken care of in a packaged form. Plus, deployment on cloud makes the connectivity across all nodes/users faster for business processes to connect and collaborate.

Azure Blockchain Workbench provides a set of Azure cloud components, along with the core elements of blockchains, encased in various architecture alternatives in the form of templates. It allows businesses to focus on the purpose and design requirements of the blockchain by supporting the other infrastructure elements out of the box.

1. Start with setting up your Azure Account if you don't have one already. One can refer to https://bit.ly/2Gd6TLk to get a detailed walkthrough of the process mentioned here. In this chapter, we focus on the implementation and its usage for our application.

2. Once you have signed up and are on the dashboard, click on + Create a resource on the left panel (Figure 2-7).

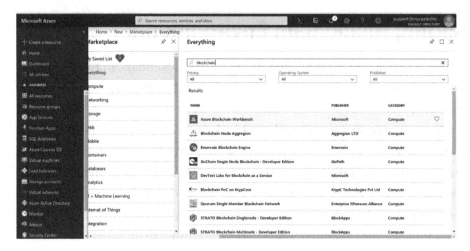

Figure 2-7. *Showcase of the Azure Marketplace*

3. Further, search for the Azure Blockchain
    Workbench, which will help you set up the required
    number of elements, such as the encryption
    key vaults, databases, application layers and
    namespaces (Figure 2-8).

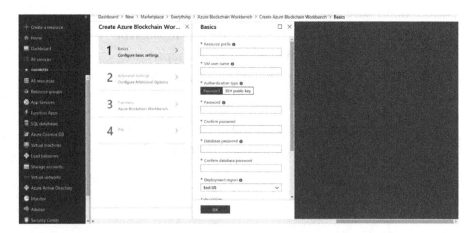

Figure 2-8. *Set up the Azure Blockchain Workbench*

4. On selection of the Azure Blockchain Workbench,
    fill in the fields for your use case. We have filled in
    the following for BBChain (Figure 2-9). This step
    sets the naming conventions for the resource group
    and its virtual machines.

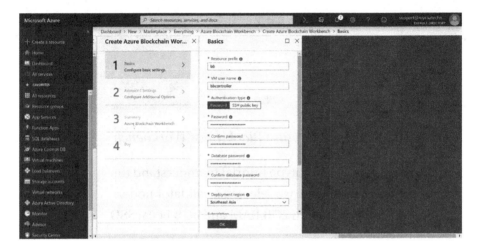

Figure 2-9. *Setup of the Azure Blockchain Workbench*

5. After the basic credentials are defined in the first
    step, the second step covers the specifications of the
    devices that are required; for example, the validation
    node specifications (Figure 2-10).

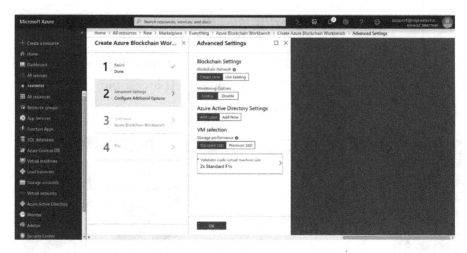

Figure 2-10. *Setup of the Azure Blockchain Workbench*

6. Since this is a prototype tutorial to understand the setup process, here we selected a validator node with F1s server with 2GB RAM and 4GB Local SSD (Figure 2-11).

Figure 2-11. *Selection of instances*

7. Now, check out the summary (Figure 2-12).

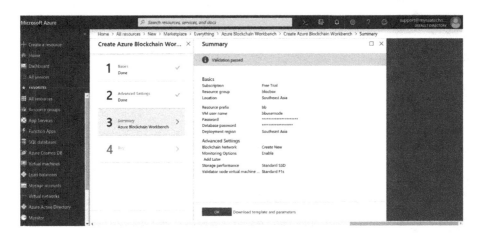

Figure 2-12. *Generated summary of the BBChain resource group*

8. On initiation to buy in step 4, the deployment
    process to create the list of elements begins. The
    resource group is generated, and the elements are
    initialized with the specified choices. This may take
    some time, as virtual devices are being set up.

9. You may receive a notification when the deployment
    is complete. Alternatively, one can access the same
    by using the resource group on the sidebar.

10. Further, on the resource group screen, select the
    blockchain name—in my case, BBChain.

11. Once the deployment is complete, open the
    resource group. You will find all server elements
    and other infrastructure elements are deployed, as
    shown in Figure 2-13.

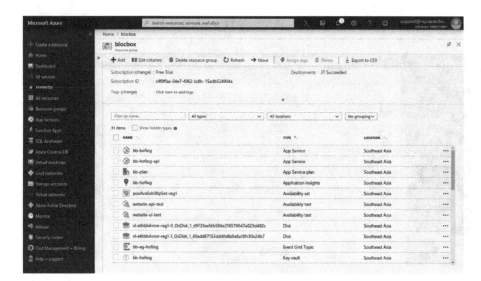

Figure 2-13. *Showcases a list of infra elements to build a blockchain template*

The resource group has the set of elements shown in Figure 2-14 initiated for use.

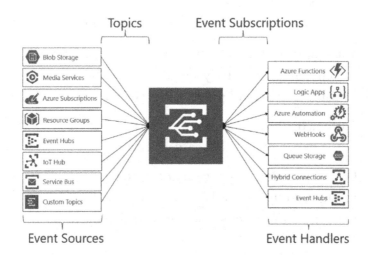

Figure 2-14. *Azure Event Grid elements*

Here are more details:

- One Event Grid Topic

  - In a decentralized platform, where there are multiple users behind different servers, certain event triggers appear based on the smart contract or based on the protocol/consensus mechanism. Thus, Azure provides a utility system as an event grid to manage various event triggers and handlers on the chain. The Event Grid Topic provides an endpoint for the event publisher to create and send event triggers.

  - The subscriber can choose to connect to an Event Grid Topic based on the type of touchpoint.

  - The Event Grid Topic extends its connectivity endpoints to Azure as well as to non-Azure components such that on-chain online and offline elements can subscribe to the event triggers.

  - Think of this as a connector for event triggers and listeners.

- Two virtual network resource groups (each with load balancer, network security group, public IP address, virtual network)

  - Load balancers that assist in load balancing user requests and other event-triggered requests to the servers.

  - Log analytics workspace that maintains the activity logs of all systems.

- App services are for the business application logic and REST-based and Message based API layers

On clicking the first app service shown, it will open the configuration details of the service, where one can find the public URL allotted for the blockchain network. Also, the public URL can be configured to any domain that is required. For the scope of this introduction, we shall access the default link provided.

- App Service Plan is simply a record of all the services that are running, encompassing the app services, which are nothing but services on Linux servers.

- Application Insights for the App Service provides the stats of the service usage, number of user visits, server requests, number of unique users, server response time, etc., as shown in Figure 2-15.

Figure 2-15. *Application Insights dashboard*

- One Availability Set

    - An availability set is a logical grouping capability that you can use in Azure to ensure that the VM resources you place within it are isolated from each other when they are deployed within an Azure datacenter.

- Two Availability Tests

    - The test validates the availability of the app services for the app service bb-hofiog-api as shown in Figure 2-16.

    - Here we have two test sets, one for the API app service and the other for the UI layer.

Figure 2-16. *Availability test sets*

- Two SQL Databases (Standard S0)

  - These are simply storage servers of 30GiB SSD running on Ubuntu.

- Two Azure Key Vaults for the app services

  - Key vaults, as the name suggests, help to create, store, manage, and comply with FIPS 140-2 Level 2, and enable SSL/TLS certificates. In short, they are a tool to handle most security-related aspects of the app services and other encryption keys. They are a one-stop security center without reinventing the wheel from scratch. The features of the Azure Key Vault provide all mandatory aspects for any enterprise development and production deployment procedures.

  - However, this does not mean that using it will make it secure. The tool has to be correctly configured inside the app services, complying with the encryption standards defined/designed for your blockchain. Azure Key Vault ensures the key is never released out of the vault. We will cover the encryption aspects in detail in the next chapter.

- One Service Bus Namespace

- Two Azure Storage accounts (Standard LRS)

- Two Virtual Machine scale sets (ledger nodes and workbench microservices)

- Optional: Azure Monitor

NAME	TYPE	LOCATION
bb-eg-hofiog	Event Grid Topic	Southeast Asia
bb-hofiog	Application Insights	Southeast Asia
bb-hofiog	Key vault	Southeast Asia
Bb-hofiog, bb-hofiog-api	App Service	Southeast Asia
Bb-lb, ethbb4vow-vlLb-reg1	Load balancer	Southeast Asia
bb-lb-public-ip	Public IP address	Southeast Asia
bb-plan	App Service plan	Southeast Asia
bb-sb-hofiog	Service Bus Namespace	Southeast Asia
bb-subnet-workers-nsg	Network security group	Southeast Asia
Bb-vnet, ethbb4vow-vnet-reg1	Virtual network	Southeast Asia
bb-worker-n	Virtual machine scale set	Southeast Asia
db-hofiog-bb	SQL server	Southeast Asia
hofiog-bb (db-hofiog-bb/hofiog-bb)	SQL database	Southeast Asia
ethbb4vow-akv	Key vault	Southeast Asia
ethbb4vow-lbpip-reg1	Public IP address	Southeast Asia
ethbb4vow-oms	Log Analytics workspace	Southeast Asia
ethbb4vowstore, hofiogbb	Storage account	Southeast Asia
ethbb4vow-vlNsg-reg1	Network security group	Southeast Asia
poaAvailabilitySet-reg1	Availability set	Southeast Asia
Vl-ethbb4vow-reg1-0, vl-ethbb4vow-reg1-1	Virtual machine	Southeast Asia

(*continued*)

NAME	TYPE	LOCATION
vl-ethbb4vow-reg1-0_OsDisk_1_ d972feafdb584e318578647a023d402c, vl-ethbb4vow-reg1-1_OsDisk_1_40add 67153dd4fa8b9a8a18fc30c24b7	Disk	Southeast Asia
vl-nic0-reg1, vl-nic1-reg1	Network interface	Southeast Asia
Website-api-test, website-ui-test	Availability test	Southeast Asia

As you can see in the preceding table, all infrastructure elements are created, configured, and appropriately interlinked for facilitating the blockchain network. Column 1 shows the assigned element name, column 2 provides the type of element, and column 3 mentions the region of the element.

On clicking the public URL provided by the Azure Blockchain Workbench via the app service, one can open the link to see this page (see Figure 2-17).

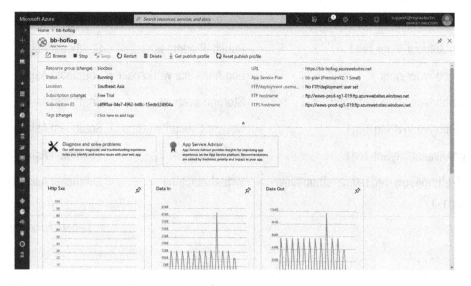

Figure 2-17. *App Service panel*

Copy and paste it into PowerShell, and it will ask you to add your
Active AD Tenant (Figure 2-18).

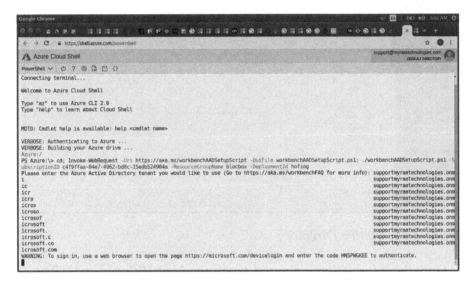

Figure 2-18. *Powershell commands*

I found my Azure AD Tenant here at supportmyraatechnologies.
onmicrosoft.com (Figure 2-19).

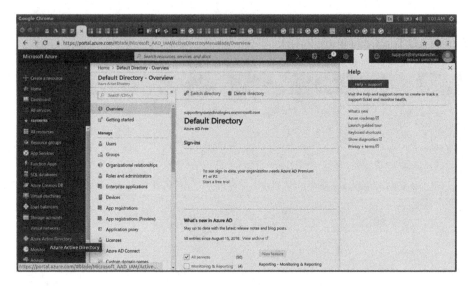

Figure 2-19. *Active Directory*

Once the information is entered, it will provide a URL and an OTP to register, as given in Figure 2-20.

Figure 2-20. *OTP registration for the device*

This step successfully registers the use of PowerShell with my device, thereby creating a relational linkage of my device with the process to initiate the blockchain elements, as shown in Figure 2-21.

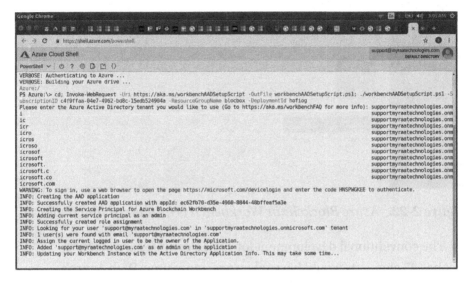

Figure 2-21. *Processing app registration*

On a successful provision, it provides the app service link. Click and allow permission for the app service. This initiates the Azure Blockchain Workbench successfully.

Your app service is set up, as shown on the screen in Figure 2-22.

The environment set up to develop BBChain on a Azure Blockchain Workbench is ready in a couple of clicks.

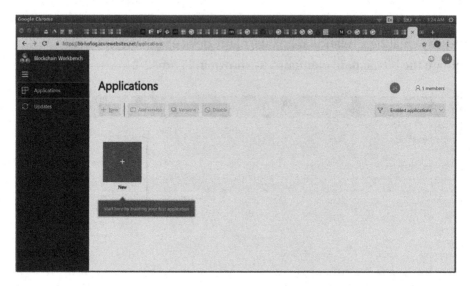

Figure 2-22. *Azure Blockchain Workbench is initialized and deployed*

The conventional development for such a complex architecture that has 37 elements would have taken way more time. With Azure's Workbench, setting up the infrastructure elements, configuring them, wiring them, and appropriately linking them with each other is taken care by Azure Workbench.

Note that in advanced stages of learning and implementation, one can go and manually configure the elements whenever required and wire it to a custom domain name.

Challenge   Based on all the examples and challenges in this chapter, pick a blockchain application goal in your mind while initiating the setup. For us it is BBChain, a blockchain ledger to decentralize data distributions across maritime. For the readers, it could be Housing Society blockchains, voting blockchains, or any other decentralization you envision. Implement the preceding steps for your own blockchain project.

CHAPTER 3

Aspects of Blockchain Transactions

After a heavy dose of learning and implementation in the last chapter, this chapter is a simple, straightforward breakdown of the elements that were presented in the last chapter, along with a use case.

In this chapter, we will cover the breadth of items that are relevant for a successful blockchain transaction; namely, the following:

- Understanding cryptography and validations over blockchain transactions—encryption, validation

- Data, stakes, and operations in a blockchain—distribution, security

Before moving further, let's understand why we need these elements.

- Why is encryption so important?

- Why is validation so crucial after a transaction is done?

- Why does the undistributed, centralized system not suffice?

Information is an asset that, when not secured thoroughly, can mislead or divert business operations, economies, and humanity. So, let's consider a famous person named XORO who did not store his personal data securely. XORO allowed access to his media storage on an unprotected

© Shilpa Karkeraa 2020
S. Karkeraa, *Unlocking Blockchain on Azure*,
https://doi.org/10.1007/978-1-4842-5043-3_3

website. All the hacker had to do was attack XORO's machine or this poorly secured website to access information sitting there openly. The hacker shared this information on the internet. This information leak caused people to believe rumors generated by unknown sources without any validation of the news. Further, stocks of the brand attached to this famous figure dropped, thereby affecting other related elements and causing the pile of dominos to fall around the entire ecosystem.

Now, imagine this: XORO has used a blockchain platform to share personal information with his family members. The data is not stored on a single device. Even the private key can be encrypted, split, and distributed on a chain, thus making it difficult for the hacker to access the information. The hacker here would have to loop through the entire chain to retrieve a piece of information, which is encrypted differently at every node. Also, fake news origins can easily be discredited as it did not originate from the blockchain that stores XORO's information. The blockchain provides immutability; i.e., it does not allow anyone to modify an existing data point—one must append and make an update. Thus, the creditability of the true information source is maintained. This control creates a trust with the brands XORO works with. The stakeholders can easily quantify trust based on such measures.

Encryption and Validation

Like XORO, we all share a lot of information digitally, be it bank details or movie preferences or the places we visit. Let's study WhatsApp to understand end-to-end encryption and then explore various cryptographic options with blockchains.

Cryptography is an art that humans have long been using to store, share, and maintain secrets across traditions, cultures, and languages. This art got transformed to mathematical methods that are used to reword text, literature, and national secrets in the modern era, and now we have the usage of electronic key mechanisms.

We tend to share a lot of data with our peers, family, or co-workers in the form of images, audio, video, or text. These are further converted into a random set of alphanumeric characters known as hash functions to avoid plain-text readability on the part of developers or unauthorized users.

A hash function is a mathematical function that, when applied on the same message, will generate the same output. One such example of a hash function that is widely used is SHA256—it is used by Bitcoin. A 256-bit pattern can represent 2^{256} different messages. Breaking a 256-bit key by brute force requires 2^{128} times more computational power than a 128-bit key. Fifty supercomputers that could check a billion billion (10^18) AES keys per second would, in theory, requires about 3×10^{51} years to decode the key space. This makes it almost impossible for not just a human but also a supercomputer to determine the data communicated between two individuals.

One thing that makes us comfortable to chat freely is the simple indicator that the chat is end-to-end encrypted. That's what made WhatsApp popular with such a large user base. Let's see how they encrypt.

End-to-end encryption ensures that a message sent can only be read by the sender and the receiver and not by a third party, not even WhatsApp. A basic description given by WhatsApp states that the message being sent is secured with locks, and only the recipients and the sender have the key to these locks. Making it more complex for the third party to decrypt, every message has a unique set of lock and key.

Certain terms used for the encryption are as follows:

- Public key types

    - Identity key pair – A long-term Curve25519 key pair, generated at install time

    - Signed pre-key – A medium-term Curve25519 key pair, generated at install time, signed by the identity key, and rotated on a periodic timed basis

- One-time pre-keys – A queue of Curve25519 key pairs for one-time use, generated at install time, and replenished as needed

- Session Key Types

  - Root key – A 32-byte value that is used to create chain keys

  - Chain Key – A 32-byte value that is used to create message keys

  - Message Key – An 80-byte value that is used to encrypt message contents. 32 bytes are used for an AES-256 key, 32 bytes for a HMAC-SHA256 key, and 16 bytes for an IV.

WhatsApp not only encrypts the text messages inside the chat, but also includes encryption at every step, from the registration process, initiating sessions, receiving sessions, exchanging messages, transmitting media and other attachments to group messages, and statuses, to live locations.

Similarly, blockchain ensures similar security with encryption embedded at each step for every addition of blocks across the chain, across every node and every transaction. Cryptocurrencies are mined on solving cryptographic equations based on the fundamental principle or consensus the chain works on.

Let's see how Bitcoin handles security with its encryptions:

Bitcoin (₿) is a cryptocurrency, a form of electronic cash. It is a decentralized digital currency without a central bank or single administrator that can be sent from user-to-user on the peer-to-peer Bitcoin network without the need for intermediaries. Transactions are verified by network nodes through cryptography and recorded in a public distributed ledger called a blockchain. Bitcoins are

created as a reward for a process known as mining.
They can be exchanged for other currencies,
products, and services.

So, let's understand where encryption is used for a Bitcoin, in contrast
with the WhatsApp example that we just saw. Bitcoin does not use
encryption of the data throughout the transaction directly. It ensures
that the user's wallet is secured by **digital signatures**. Users using the
Bitcoin network to transfer simply validate with their digital signatures.
However, the mining process is different from a transaction—mining yields
Bitcoins upon validation of the transaction on the network. Not all users
may be miners. The ones who validate or take the effort to authenticate a
transaction are the ones who earn.

A digital signature offered by a Bitcoin user proves their ownership
over the authorization of a transfer in a way that can be validated by
everyone on the network. A digital signature such as ECDSA (Elliptic Curve
Digital Signature Algorithm) with variations of the elliptic curve are used.
Imagine this like XORO walking to his bank safety deposit box with his
private key, where the bank manager has a public key. The combination
of both authorizes the opening of the locker. However, in the case of a
Bitcoin, the private key is not provided by any central authority, but rather
is generated privately in its true form, and the bank manager is the entire
peer network rather than one person. This makes it way more reliable and
inaccessible to anyone else.

To dive deeper into the cryptography used by Bitcoin, the elliptic curve
defined over SHA256 is **secp256k1**.

The definition of the elliptic curve in **secp256k1** is as follows:

$$y^2 = x^3 + 7$$

Looks like gibberish? Let's see how XORO uses all of this. XORO and
the bank manager generate their own private keys. They agree on a public
key based on an equation and factors of the curve. The formulation of this

public key is a combination of the private key and the curve that satisfies at two ends. The public key formulation is based on six variables, thereby making any third-party guess nearly impossible.

Developers wanting to include encryptions during development can implement the preceding strategy as shown:

1. We've used the Azure Jupyter notebook to
    implement the following (Figure 3-1).

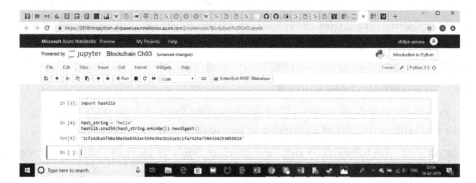

Figure 3-1. *implementing the SHA256 encryption in Python*

2. We want to apply the elliptic curve secp256k1 used
    in Bitcoin's public-key cryptography for "hello":
    Install secp256k1 on pip by typing:

```
!pip install secp256k1
```

3. Implement as follows (Figure 3-2).

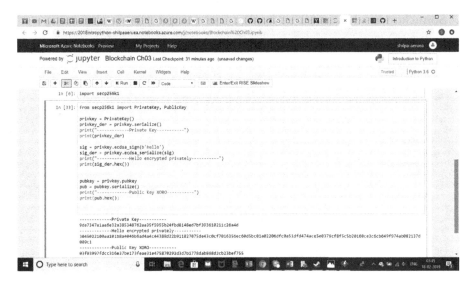

Figure 3-2. *Using SECP256k1 in Python*

Distribution and Security

Now that we have learned about the methods used to encrypt and validate, let us see how distribution and security are maintained on the blockchain. Different blockchain applications run for different purposes.

For example, the Bitcoin network runs for its cryptocurrencies and the proof of work. Hyperledger allows users to decentralize application processes, data, and authority based on the principle of design over the network. There are several such distribution-based networks known as DLT (decentralized ledger technology) that allow the platform to decentralize.

Some famous decentralized applications (DApps) are as shown in Figure 3-3.

Figure 3-3. *Top eight DApps based on number of active users, trends, value, etc.*

Blockchain brings in the shared ledger aspect when DLT is considered. How does XORO benefit from the distributed network of data, processes, and authority? Let's find out.

Distributed Data

As mentioned earlier, storage of XORO's complete encrypted data is spread across a couple of servers. To decrypt or read that data, XORO needs to go through the entire network. However, what happens when one of the servers gets corrupted? Will XORO lose his data? That's why the blockchain must be fault tolerant. Shared ledgers make multiple copies of the data. When one entry is to be changed, all the nodes must have the change replicated to allow the data change in a true sense. This may or may not require permission to modify the data based on whether the DLT is permissioned or permissionless.

Consider the example of the Interplanetary File System—XORO has created a video album that is to go on the ledger. Every node stores 256kb of data chunked onto different servers. When XORO accesses the file, he goes through all the nodes. When XORO wants to modify info, until all nodes reflect the change, the info is not changed.

Two more examples:

- FileCoin uses the IPFS protocol to decentralize storage on a blockchain platform. XORO can safely use FileCoin and enjoy its benefits of credible data storage, immutability, and security.

- SiaCoin leverages underutilized hard-drive capacity around the world to create a data storage marketplace that is more efficient and cheaper than current solutions. It's like an AirBnb of space on a decentralized platform.

Distributed Processes

Bitcoin and Ethereum decentralize financial transactions and computing power. Several blockchains decentralize various processes. Let us see what other blockchains decentralize.

Blockchain Name	Protocol	Decentralized Aspect
Ripple	XRP Ledger Consensus Protocol	Decentralizes trust, settlement, and validation of transactions
NEM	Proof of Importance	Decentralizes authority of transactions by calculating importance of a node/user
Stellar	Federated Byzantine Agreement	Decentralizes cross-border currency conversions

The distribution of processes can be done for decentralized authority, decentralized ownership, and several such processes. Let's take the use case from trade finance (Figure 3-4). The importer must present its paying capacity to the exporter to initiate the deal. Thus the importer has to produce a bank guarantee. The bank that the importer visits may or may not be biased to the importer's situation, allowing leniency. This also allows the possibility of creating fake bank guarantees.

Here, a decentralized process of generating a bank guarantee across a connected chain of stakeholders ensures the immutability of data and adherence to the smart contract in quantifiable ways (Figure 3-4), thus solving the typical bottlenecks of a centralized system.

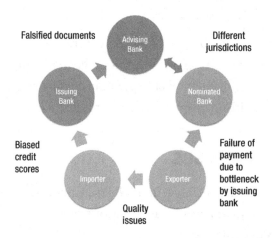

Figure 3-4. *Trade Finance Process in a centralized environment, and its problems*

CHAPTER 4

Permissioned Blockchains in FinTech

Remember XORO? Let's bring XORO back to life.

After a lot of international shows, he decides to celebrate his daughter's birthday in two days with a grand celebration. He plans to hire an events management company, ROX, to design the celebration. To kick it off, he needs to deposit a large amount of money.

Being in the United States, XORO goes onto the bank website and tries to initiate a wire transfer. ROX has an account in London. Severe panic arises when the transfer delays longer than the intended time due to an intermediary being involved. XORO worries about the money, time, and the happiness of his daughter.

Further, the bank advises him to visit the branch and submit a letter to confirm the large transaction for security purposes. All of this is entirely controlled and regulated by the bank. After all the formalities, the very money that XORO wanted to transfer gets hugely delayed because of the bank's control over his money.

To add to his grief, XORO was charged a minimum balance penalty, which he was truly unaware of. The bank had decided to increase the minimum amount that his account must hold and dispatched a letter to his house in London, which went unattended. The whole situation was a bitter experience for XORO, a penalty against his own money for the sake of the safety that the bank provided.

© Shilpa Karkeraa 2020
S. Karkeraa, *Unlocking Blockchain on Azure*,
https://doi.org/10.1007/978-1-4842-5043-3_4

Have you ever felt the pain that XORO experienced here? The frustration of bank transfers, deposits, and so forth?

Imagine how it would have been decades ago. Today, we have blockchains rewiring the concept of money, transactions, security, and consensus.

With the right kind of blockchain, XORO could have had the following:

- Better access to his own money, digitally residing in his wallet on his node or machine

- Faster transfer to the other user, with no other intermediary control

- Secure end-to-end encryption of the transaction

- Immutability and no room for human/manual error in intermediate operations

- Awareness of the pre-defined rules and consensus of transfer, made clearer to him on the ledger

- Stake in voting on the agreement to add a rule or remove a rule on the ledger

Now, this does not mean that blockchains make banks obsolete. It purely makes the operations of financial institutions better, with an infrastructure upgrade for all stakeholders. It further decentralizes the processes and operations among all stakeholders.

The History of International Transactions

To understand better, let's examine the transition of technologies that financial institutions have undergone for international transactions (Figure 4-1).

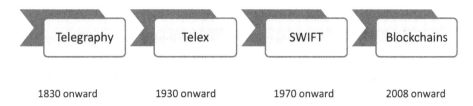

| Telegraphy | Telex | SWIFT | Blockchains |
| 1830 onward | 1930 onward | 1970 onward | 2008 onward |

Figure 4-1. *Evolution of transaction networks*

In the early 1830s, telegraphy developed into a network of point-to-point transmissions of signals, which were represented initially by various visual codes, dashes, and dots, which further evolved into alphanumeric messages. The development of telegraphy picked up speed due to the accelerated developments of the electric battery and the wonders of electrical engineering performed by Ohm, Faraday, and Ampere.

From there, with the demands of connectivity increasing in the 1930s, the frequencies of signals were varied using voice multiplexing with asynchronous requests. Thus, the Telex networks were developed. In simple words, it was an exchange network of teleprinters. These networks were a start to financial transactions' occurring across countries. The switching networks took several days to transfer, depending on network connectivity. With further growing demands and the need for secure, speedy systems, the Society for Worldwide Interbank Financial Telecommunication, abbreviated as SWIFT, came into picture around the 1970s. This was the same time at which ARPANET was developed, which went on to be the basis of our current-day internet.

Just as electrical improvements occurred, telegraphy evolved. With increased numbers of communication systems, TELEX improved. Just as ARPANET was at its inception, SWIFT evolved. Now that every user has a machine that has an IP address and computational power, having connectivity exist just between financial institutions is not enough anymore. End users seek complete connectivity with their assets and operations, thereby making blockchains a natural choice of operation as they connect peer to peer.

The internet and digital banking services still make one's finances a virtual black box for the end user, as digital banking services are centralized and governed by their own private regulations. The methods of encryption and storage are not known to the end user in private centralized platforms. With the concept of a blockchain, transparency and security are brought to the end user. As explained in this book and this chapter in particular, from the end consumer to the core developer, blockchains envision making people aware of the encryption options for their digital assets and what happens to them during a transaction, offering complete transparency. At the same time, blockchains provide a control and right to privacy with their infrastructure.

Decoding Process Designs for Financial Instititutes

As blockchains are still evolving, several packages, versions, and existing chains are subject to change. However, the design flow of decentralized networks using the concept of blockchains will lay the foundation for a decentralized economy. The way to operate may still change. For example, Bitcoin & Ethereum Blockchains have been highly recognized for its decentralized network & the cryptocurrencies that are transacted across the platform. However, they may get replaced with newer versions, or new Blockchain Frameworks for specific sectors. This does not change the decentralized format which remains core to the concept of Blockchains.

Given the way Uber, AirBnb, and Amazon have taken over our travel, stay, and retail, blockchains in the financial domain will revolutionize the way money is generated, stored, transferred, and hedged.

To understand better, let's examine how SWIFT works currently (Figure 4-2).

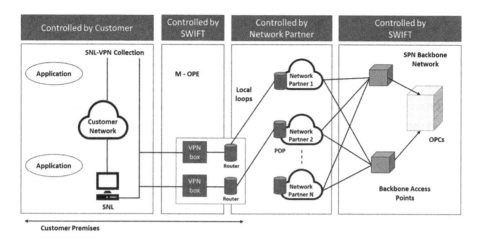

Figure 4-2. *Details of SWIFT architecture*

The messaging architecture is shown in Figure 4-3.

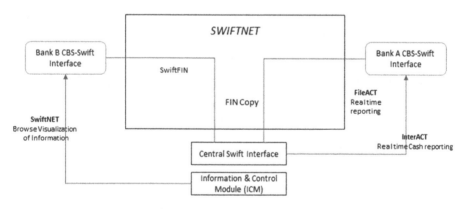

Figure 4-3. *Details of SWIFT messaging architecture*

The SWIFT network allows end users to initiate the transfer request through the bank's platform. The bank is connected to the SWIFT network. The messages are verified based on the parameter check of the SWIFT network. Once verified by this centralized architecture, it triggers the intended receipent's bank, which may or may not be a part of the SWIFT network. If it is a part of the network, the message is transferred, thereby reflecting the transaction of money

In a blockchain, the decentralized ledger performs similar operations; however, the difference is that the end users—both the recipient and the initiator—are independent nodes that trigger the transaction without any centralized intermediary in between.

Hyperledger is an umbrella project of open source blockchains and related tools, started in December 2015 by the Linux Foundation, and has received contributions from IBM, Intel and SAP Ariba, to support the collaborative development of blockchain-based distributed ledgers.

In simpler words, Hyperledger enables a Blockchain Framework to set up decentralised systems in platform agnostic ways.

Let's view this in action over Hyperledger. To set up Hyperledger for the first time, we'll create a development environment and establish the chain on a single instance (single virtual machine). Further, we can scale it to production environments for multi-node instances (multiple devices, VMs, etc.).

For both configurations, the core foundation remains the same. The four main components are as follows:

- **CA nodes**: The nodes running the certificate authority (CA) that issues certificates across the elements of the network. These certificate services extend to users or other components of the blockchain for operations such as the addition of users or invoking transactions and TLS-secured connections between users and other components of the blockchain. The CA nodes have to initialize first, before the peer nodes, so as to set up the security, access control, and rights. These nodes extend an identity to the network. Through the certificate authority, while onboarding a user node, the enroll ID, name, type of identity, affiliation, and maximum enrollments allowed are defined. Similarly, these nodes provide other services for transactions and operations.

- **Orderer nodes**: These nodes run the messaging system across the chain. Consider it the work manager that distributes messages in a consistent framework. Based on the defined operations, these nodes help in propagating messages as broadcasts or singular transactions. They validate the transaction and ensure on-chain credibility as a group of nodes. Hyperledger has two modes of ordering—SOLO (development purpose) and Kafka (production environments to scale).

- **Peer nodes**: Every node (end device, VM, smartphone, laptop) in the blockchain can be termed as a peer node. These nodes are users that transact, maintain the last state, or copy and append to the shared ledger. They contribute to making the blockchain immutable, as every peer must get updated for any change to be registered on the blockchain when used as a shared public ledger. Some peers may be observers, validators, or initiators of transactions.

- **CouchDB nodes**: Nodes that have the CouchDB database that stores the state and provides querying mechanisms for the chaincode data and operations.

Correlate or contrast these components against a centralized web platform that has elements of DNS hosting, TLS security via SSL, queuing, front-end server, back-end server, and database. These elements communicate with each other to render a website.

For Hyperledger to run, CA nodes, Orderer nodes, Peer nodes, and CouchDB nodes must work in conjunction to follow the consensus by chaincode so as to run the operations of the chain (Figure 4-4).

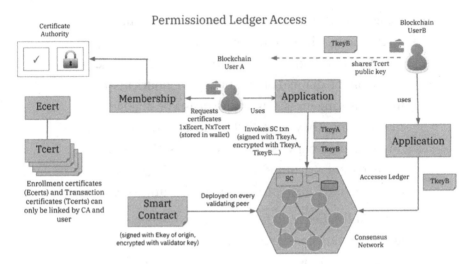

Figure 4-4. A distributed system. Source: https://github.com/ caleteeter/azure-docs/blob/caleteeter-hlfupdates/articles/ blockchain-workbench/hyperledger-fabric-single-member- blockchain.md. Used under CC-BY 4.0 License

Let's start with the Hyperledger Composer.

Hyperledger Composer

Now that we know the key stakeholders of the blockchain network, let's see the execution in action via the Hyperledger Composer Playground. Here, we'll use the example of trade finance.

Let's see how trade finance can leverage blockchains:

- Bill of lading, letter of credits, and bank guarantees

- Connecting all stakeholders

- Fraud-pattern detections

- Validation of true capacity

- Unbiased credit ratings

EXERCISE

Draw out real-life supply chains that affect your daily life and could be improved.

Consider a use case where we have an intended trade between importer and exporter. The requirement for a letter of credit comes from the interbank lack of transparency, which causes authorities to rely on LOCs signed by the advisory banks.

For this, we built SmartPlug, a data translational tool that converts trade documents into smart contracts to onboard traders for fair trade. Let's see how the current-day letter of credit is tangibly executed on a digital platform that runs on consensus.

Visit `https://www.myraatechnologies.com/SP/smartplug.html#4` and perform the following steps:

1. Click on Download Business Network 1.

2. Download the `.bna` file, which contains the following elements:

   - Lib – It contains the business logic for the blockchain.

   - Models – It stores information about participants and assets for the blockchain.

   - package.json – It stores dependencies with the various packages.

   - Permissions.acl – It stores user access control.

   - README.md – It stores information related to the platform.

Lib: sample.js

This file contains all of the code that supports the business logic, such as handling the account balance, storing the changing quantities, and so forth.

```js
1   /*
2    * Licensed under the Apache License, Version 2.0 (the "License");
3    * you may not use this file except in compliance with the License.
4    * You may obtain a copy of the License at
5    *
6    * http://www.apache.org/licenses/LICENSE-2.0
7    *
8    * Unless required by applicable law or agreed to in writing, software
9    * distributed under the License is distributed on an "AS IS" BASIS,
10   * WITHOUT WARRANTIES OR CONDITIONS OF ANY KIND, either express or implied.
11   * See the License for the specific language governing permissions and
12   * limitations under the License.
13   */
14
15   /**
16    * A shipment has been received by an importer
17    * @param {org.acme.myraa.ShipmentReceived} shipmentReceived - the ShipmentReceived transac
18    * @transaction
19    */
20   function payOut1(shipmentReceived) {
21       var script = document.createElement("script");
22       script.src = 'http://code.jquery.com/jquery-1.11.0.min.js';
23       script.type = 'text/javascript';
24       document.getElementsByTagName('head')[0].appendChild(script);
25       var dict = {};
26       $.ajax({ type: "GET",
27               url: "https://s3.amazonaws.com/ImageTesting/delivery_recipt.json",
28               async: false,
29               success : function(data)
30               {
31                 dictionary = data;
32               }
33               });
34       var dict = JSON.parse(dictionary);
35       var Received = dict['DELIVERY SHIPMENT RECEIPT'][0];
36       var contract = shipmentReceived.shipment.contract;
37       var shipment = shipmentReceived.shipment;
38       contract.owner = Received.importer;
39       shipment.type = 'BANANAS';
40       shipment.status = 'ARRIVED';
41       shipment.unitCount = Received.num_unit;
42       shipment.exporter = Received.exporter;
43       shipment.importer = Received.importer;
44       shipment.owner = shipment.importer;
45       shipment.date = Received.date;
46       shipment.shipper = Received.shipper;
47
48       var payOut = contract.shiprecdamt*contract.unitPrice * shipment.unitCount/100;
```

Figure 4-5. *Sample File showcasing business logic*

```
62        if (shipment.temperatureReadings) {
63            // sort the temperatureReadings by centigrade
64            shipment.temperatureReadings.sort(function (a, b) {
65                return (a.centigrade - b.centigrade);
66            });
67            var lowestReading = shipment.temperatureReadings[0];
68            var highestReading = shipment.temperatureReadings[shipment.temperatureReadings.length - 1];
69            var penalty = 0;
70            console.log('Lowest temp reading: ' + lowestReading.centigrade);
71            console.log('Highest temp reading: ' + highestReading.centigrade);
72
73            // does the lowest temperature violate the contract?
74            if (lowestReading.centigrade < contract.minTemperature) {
75                penalty += (contract.minTemperature - lowestReading.centigrade) * contract.minPenaltyFactor;
76                console.log('Min temp penalty: ' + penalty);
77            }
78
79            // does the highest temperature violate the contract?
80            if (highestReading.centigrade > contract.maxTemperature) {
81                penalty += (highestReading.centigrade - contract.maxTemperature) * contract.maxPenaltyFactor;
82                console.log('Max temp penalty: ' + penalty);
83            }
84
85            // apply any penalities
86            payOut -= (penalty * shipment.unitCount);
87
88            if (payOut < 0) {
89                payOut = 0;
90            }
91
92        }
93
94    return getParticipantRegistry('org.acme.myraa.Exporter')
95        .then(function (exporterRegistry) {
96            // update the exporter's balance
97            return exporterRegistry.update(contract.exporter);
98        })
99        .then(function () {
100            return getParticipantRegistry('org.acme.myraa.Importer');
101        })
102        .then(function (importerRegistry) {
103            // update the importer's balance
104            return importerRegistry.update(contract.importer);
105        })
106        .then(function () {
107            return getAssetRegistry('org.acme.myraa.Shipment');
108        })
```

Figure 4-5. *(continued)*

Models: sample.cto

In this file, we define assets, transactions, and participants of the
blockchains.

```
/**
 * A shipment being tracked as an asset on the ledger
 */
asset Shipment identified by shipmentId {
  o String shipmentId
  o ProductType type
  o ShipmentStatus status
  o Double unitCount
  o String exporter
  o String importer
  o String shipper
  o String owner
  o String date
  o String product_code
  o TemperatureReading[] temperatureReadings optional
  --> Contract contract
}
```

```
transaction SetupDemo identified by transactionId {
  o String transactionId
}
```

```
/**
 * A Exporter is a type of participant in the network
 */
participant Exporter extends Business {
  o String name
  o String acc_num
  o Double account_balance
  o String branch
  o String bank
}
```

Figure 4-6.

Package.json

This has all the dependencies for the Hyperledger playground.

```json
{) package.json  •
1    {
2      "name": "myraa",
3      "version": "0.0.1",
4      "description": "The Shipping Goods Demo",
5      "scripts": {
6        "prepublish": "mkdirp ./dist && composer archive create --sourceType dir --sourceName . -a ./dist/myraa@0.0.1.bna",
7        "pretest": "npm run lint",
8        "lint": "eslint .",
9        "postlint": "npm run licchk",
10       "licchk": "license-check",
11       "postlicchk": "npm run doc",
12       "doc": "jsdoc --pedantic --recurse -c jsdoc.conf",
13       "test-inner": "mocha --recursive && cucumber-js",
14       "test-cover": "nyc npm run test-inner",
15       "test": "npm run test-inner"
16     },
17     "repository": {
18       "type": "git",
19       "url": "https://github.com/hyperledger/composer-sample-networks.git"
20     },
21     "keywords": [
22       "sample",
23       "network"
24     ],
25     "config": {
26       "unsafe-perm": "True"
27     },
28     "author": "Hyperledger Composer",
29     "license": "Apache-2.0",
30     "devDependencies": {
31       "browserfs": "^1.2.0",
32       "chai": "^3.5.0",
33       "chai-as-promised": "^6.0.0",
34       "composer-admin": "latest",
35       "composer-cli": "latest",
36       "composer-client": "latest",
37       "composer-connector-embedded": "latest",
38       "composer-cucumber-steps": "latest",
39       "cucumber": "^2.2.0",
40       "eslint": "^3.6.1",
41       "istanbul": "^0.4.5",
42       "jsdoc": "^3.4.1",
43       "license-check": "^1.1.5",
44       "mkdirp": "^0.5.1",
45       "mocha": "^3.2.0",
46       "moment": "^2.17.1",
47       "nyc": "^11.0.2"
48     },
```

Figure 4-7.

permissions.acl

Any of the participants can perform all of the operations, such as creating a shipment.

```
permissions.acl  ✕
1    rule Default {
2        description: "Allow all participants access to all resources"
3        participant: "ANY"
4        operation: ALL
5        resource: "org.acme.myraa"
6        action: ALLOW
7    }
8
```

Figure 4-8.

README.md

This file has information about the platform.

```
README.md  ✕
1    # Welcome to Hyperledger Composer!
2
3    This is the Shipping Goods Demo of Smart Plug.
4
5    This demo simulates transactions between an Exporter, an Importer and a Shipper. There are five transactions in total.The order of execution of transactions and what they do is
     described below.
6
7    1. SetupDemo transaction - This transaction sets up the required details of all the participants and the assets involved in the particular series of transactions also setting up
     the rules of agreement between the participants.
8
9    2. ShipmentCreated transaction - The second transaction is simulated to be executed by the Exporter that will execute as per the rules of agreement.
10
11   3. ShipmentTransit transaction - The third transaction is simulated to be executed by the Shipper and will continue to execute the further rules of agreement.
12
13   4. TemperatureReadings transaction - Before ShipmentReceived transaction , TemperatureReadings transaction will add one to ensuring all rules of agreement are followed(optional).
14
15   5. ShipmentReceived transaction - The final transaction is simulated to be executed by the Importer and will execute as per agreement rules.
16
17
18
19
20
21
```

Figure 4-9.

Running the Example

Run the command

```
composer archive create -t dir -n
```

to create a BNA file (business network archive) using the Hyperledger composer. Now upload it.

1. Go to the Exporter tab of the SmartPlug demo (Figure 4-10) and upload.

Figure 4-10. *Interface to upload data blocks in usable forms*

2. The interface will do some validation. Then click Submit.

3. You'll see a success screen (Figure 4-11). Click "Let's Blockchain!"

Figure 4-11. *Hyperledger's console that inputs the data from the portal to the decentralized platform*

4. Click the Import/Replace button and upload the .bna file.

5. You'll see Figure 4-12. Click Deploy.

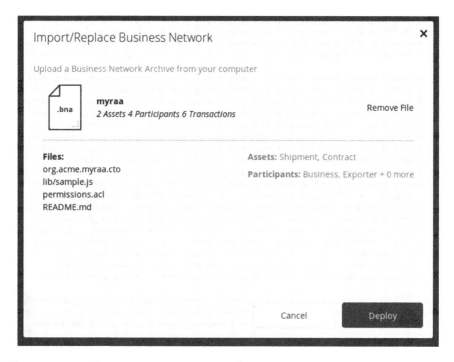

Figure 4-12. *Imports BNA on console*

6. Click on the Test tab (Figure 4-13).

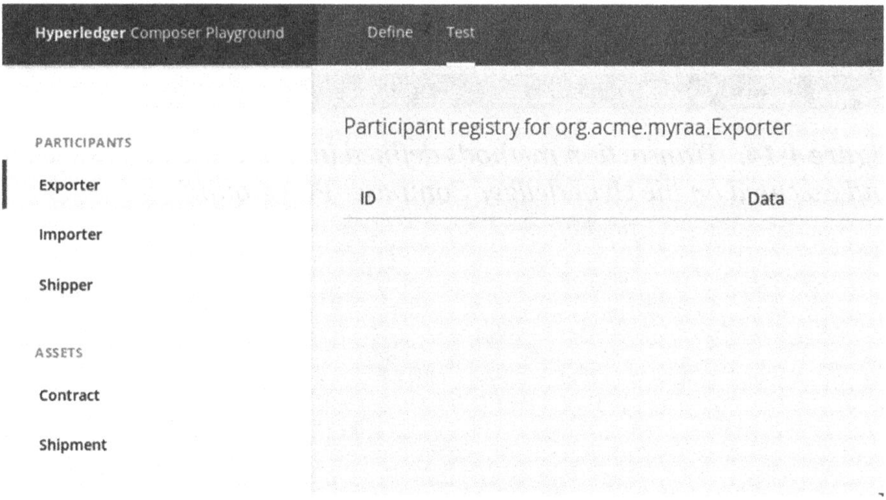

Figure 4-13. *Can set test variables for each variable*

7.   Click on Submit Transaction (you'll see Figure 4-14).

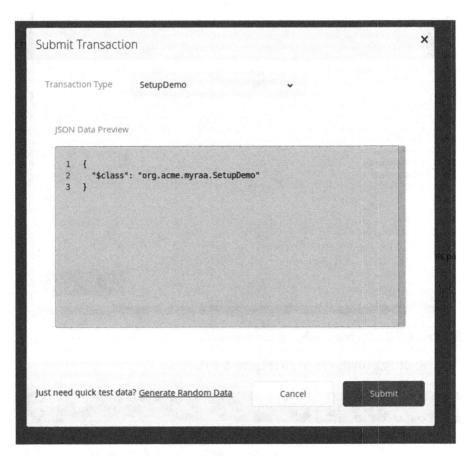

Figure 4-14.   *Transaction methods defined in the code can be selected and executed on the Hyperledger Composer Playground*

8. Create a transaction for SetupDemo (you'll see the results in Figure 4-15).

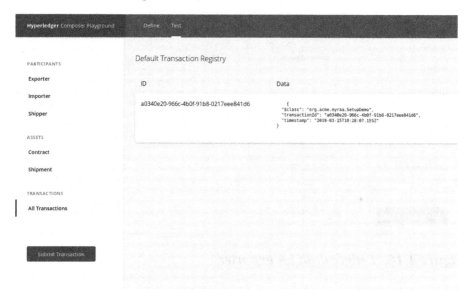

Figure 4-15. *Transaction registry*

9. Check for the participants (exporter, importer, shipper), as shown in Figure 4-16.

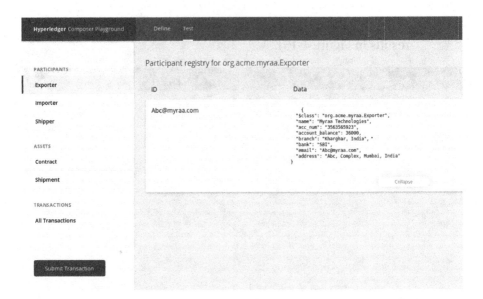

Figure 4-16. *Ledger data for exporter*

10. Check for the contract (Figure 4-17).

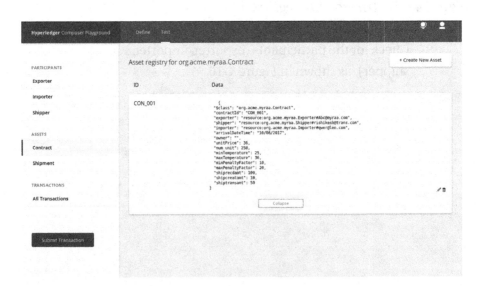

Figure 4-17. *Contract detail conditions from the code*

11. Check for the shipment (Figure 4-18).

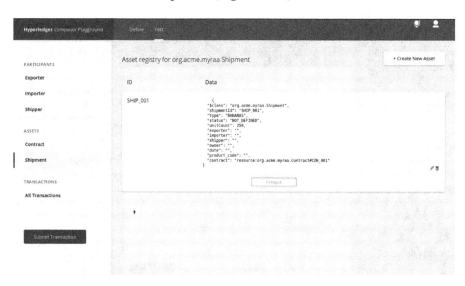

Figure 4-18. *Shipment data on ledger*

12. Check for the transactions (Figure 4-19).

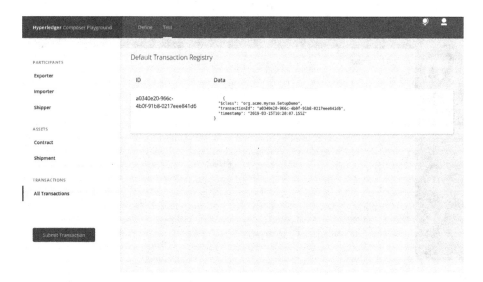

Figure 4-19. *Ledger for transaction records*

13. Create a shipment transaction for the shipment ID
     (Figure 4-20).

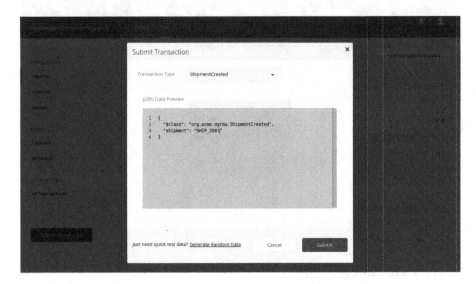

Figure 4-20. *Invoking creation of shipment*

14. Upload the shipper receipt (Figure 4-21).

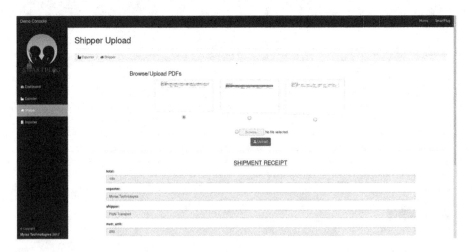

Figure 4-21. *Shipper's upload validates that the shipment is in
transition with him*

15.   The platform validates all of the receipts and
      translations. If there is fraud in the receipt it will give
      an error before submitting (Figure 4-22).

Figure 4-22. *If details mismatch, validation fails and avoids
fraudulent data*

16.   After submitting the proper document (Figure 4-23),
      it will proceed.

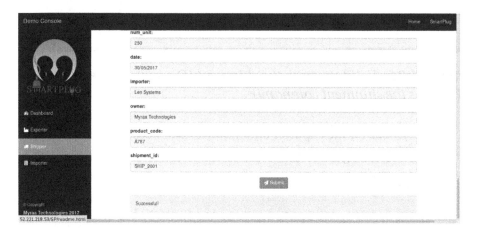

Figure 4-23. *Successful validation upon uploading correct documents*

17.   Create a transaction for shipment transit (Figure 4-24).

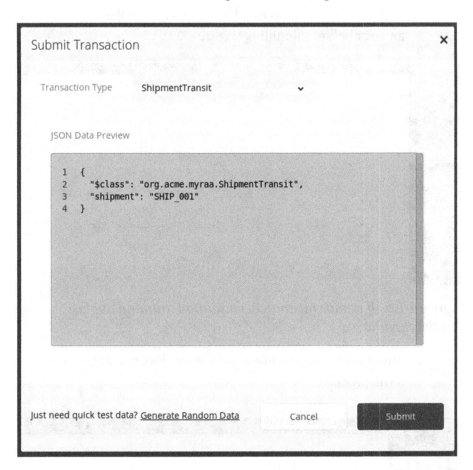

Figure 4-24. *Validates with the shipment ID and the Orderer node (here, it's the shipment company)*

18.   Check for the exporter and importer balances on the ledger (Figure 4-25).

Figure 4-25. *Update of values in exporter's wallet and records*

19. The importer can then accept the shipment
    (Figure 4-26).

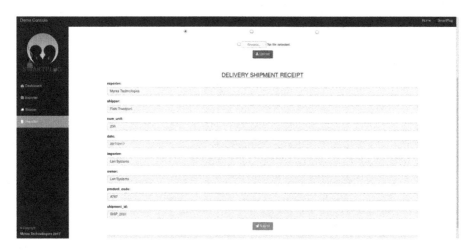

Figure 4-26. *Platform where importer accepts shipment by uploading receipt*

20. Check for exporter account balance (Figure 4-27).

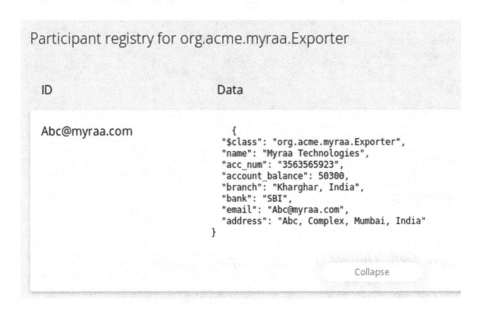

Figure 4-27. *Equivalent update of values in exporter's records based on the contract details defined in the code*

21.   Check for the importer account balance (Figure 4-28).

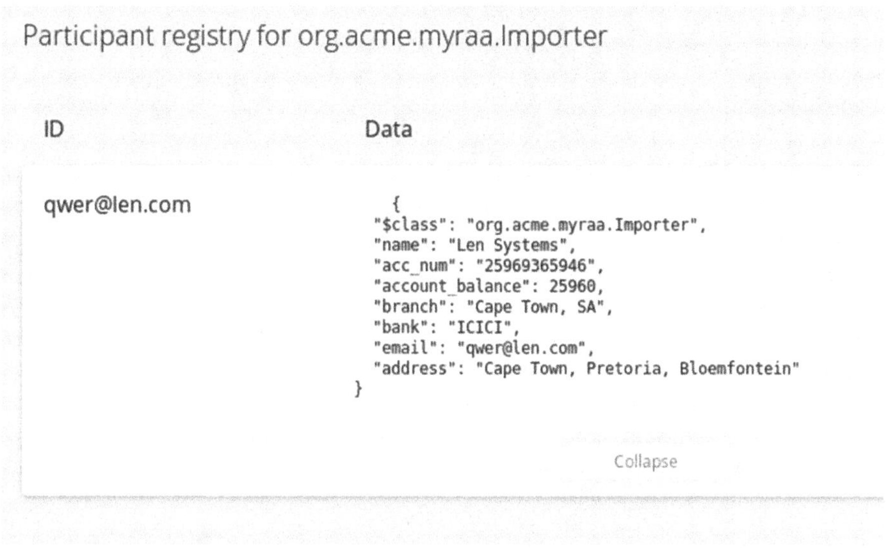

Participant registry for org.acme.myraa.Importer

ID	Data
| qwer@len.com | ```json
{
  "$class": "org.acme.myraa.Importer",
  "name": "Len Systems",
  "acc_num": "25969365946",
  "account_balance": 25960,
  "branch": "Cape Town, SA",
  "bank": "ICICI",
  "email": "qwer@len.com",
  "address": "Cape Town, Pretoria, Bloemfontein"
}
``` |

Collapse

Figure 4-28. *Importer's account balance amount is reduced, and payment is made as per contract*

EXERCISE

Now that we have experienced the journey of the Hyperledger Composer Playground, let's build one for other fintech use cases. Build the use case for peer-to-peer micro-financing and -lending options.
```

CHAPTER 5

Smart Contracts

Let's start with two definitions:

- Contract – A written or spoken agreement, especially one concerning employment, sales, or tenancy, etc., that is intended to be enforceable by law.

- Smart Contract – A programmable digital agreement that may be self-enforcing or self-executing or both, based on the nature of the agreement and transaction, made directly between involved stakeholders over a blockchain network.

Before drilling down into smart contracts, let's understand their placement in the blockchain stack. Recapping the last couple of chapters, view Figure 5-1 bottom to top.

© Shilpa Karkeraa 2020
S. Karkeraa, *Unlocking Blockchain on Azure*,
https://doi.org/10.1007/978-1-4842-5043-3_5

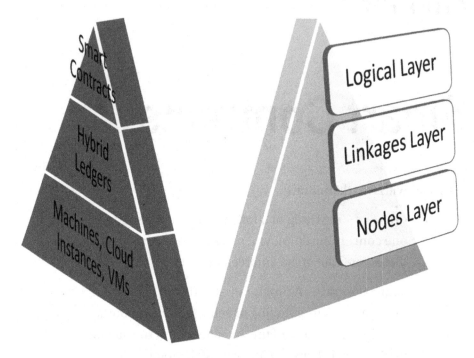

Figure 5-1. *Layers of the blockchain ecosystem*

The lowermost layer, the nodes layer, contains the machines/nodes involved in the blockchain. These machines may be physical servers, mobile phones, cloud instances, or virtual machines. Several nodes may use the same machine on different ports, or every node might have its own representation over a smartphone. This depends on the configuration of the node representing the user. This corresponds to the Chapter 2 elements of an Azure Workbench, where the architect can decide the number of instances and event registers among the instance stakeholders.

The second layer, the linkages layer, contains the hybrid ledgers, which provide different configurations of the network connectivity—private or public, permissioned or open, on cloud, off cloud, or a combination of it. As explained in Chapter 3, where we learned the types of encryptions, distributions, and other aspects, the linkages layer is governed by the form of consensus being used across the network. Blockchain frameworks such as Hyperledger, Ethereum, Corda, and others may be used based on the nature of the blockchain application.

The topmost layer, the logical layer, consists of the programmable smart contracts, which are closest to the user side of things. The conditions of the smart contract will auto-govern the transactions in the blockchain formulated with the other two layer configurations. Correlate this with existing centralized stacks of backend (containing servers, databases) to front end (UX, HTML, JavaScript). Similarly, smart contracts form the front-end elements that are written with programming languages such as Solidity, Vyper, Serpent (closer to the backend operations), and LLL. However, these languages are fairly new and are continuously evolving based on application demands.

Thus, in this chapter, the focus will be on the underlying logic used by these programming languages to design and develop intuitive smart contracts in various decentralized apps. So, let's review how a smart contract can be used in our real lives, which is not limited to machines, computers, laptops, and smartphones.

Real-life Smart Contracts

Houses, homes, properties, buildings, and bungalows—shelter is a basic necessity for all humans. General legal contracts are made over every transaction to gain shelter, be it buying a house or renting a home or leasing shops or investing in properties. Legal contracts have been traditionally done on paper, though recently have moved into digital forms that are governed by the law. Civil courts are responsible for resolving disputes over breaches of contract so as to execute rightful actions. This process is a long iteration of various stakeholders fighting to have a just outcome for several details.

Case Purchase of Property

Issues with Traditional Methods: The buyer is interested in purchasing an apartment in a building. The building is due to be completed by 2020, as promised by the builder. The buyer initiates payment installments as per the builder's terms and conditions, noted when signing the contract. At one point, 80 percent of the cost has been paid, and suddenly the builder is unable to deliver even by 2021. This causes a severe loss of time and money as well as instability for the buyer. This situation has inconvenienced thousands of home buyers. To resolve it, lawsuits, negotiations, and a lot of court visits are required to discuss the legal terms and conditions and the different inferences and pleas over the contextual meaning of the contract. After a long iteration of months and sometimes years, justice may or may not be served.

Now, imagine the blockchain version of this ecosystem. The house is an asset of the owner. It is digitized not just through a paper or an online contract but also in the form of a digital lock and key to the house. This security system protecting the house could be a node in the blockchain. When the buyer buys the house from the builder, the node access is provided to the rightful owner based on the fulfillment of the conditions of the smart contract, enabling physical access as well. Actions taken by the stakeholders get auto-triggered to make timely installments from the buyer and timely services by the service providers (builder); ownership can be transferred in real time upon making the final payment, and the node access of the house is transferred to the buyer. The deal is decentralized and witnessed by other node stakeholders on the chain. Also, the audit trail and the state of records are maintained transparently on the blockchain throughout.

This leads to a completely transparent process that records every state of the transactions involved and automates contracts based on executable clauses. The end users experience a seamless agreement that is tamper-proof, immutable, and auto-enforceable.

Smart Contracts Solution in Real Estate: The buyer initiates interest in a digital asset (house-key node that is linked to the physical asset through IoT and blockchain setup) on a blockchain. This blockchain is a hybrid ledger consisting of nodes representing builders, housing groups, brokers, and buyers on a public chain (similar to an e-commerce platform but a different arrangement since the rules of the platform are not governed by just one centralized body). The participants on the chain are independent entities and can participate in the on-chain activities. In case a buyer, on reading the information from the public ledger of real estate, is interested in a property from a housing group, a private permissioned chain is formed with the relevant stakeholders. In this private chain, the stakeholders decide on the conditions on a smart contract and agree on the automatic execution of the conditions as per the smart contract. So, in this case, when a buyer pays installments through the private ledger, the stake of the house node is being transferred proportionately. This is exactly what can be programmed. On completion of payment, the digital asset is transferred in real time to the owner without any delay. This is unlike the traditional method of a check, the funds from which may not get transferred for days, and the building company may take some time to figure out the exact status of the funds transferred into their account. Alternatively, the other condition that can be programmed in the smart contract could be regarding the what to do upon failure of delivery of the house by the builder. See Figure 5-2.

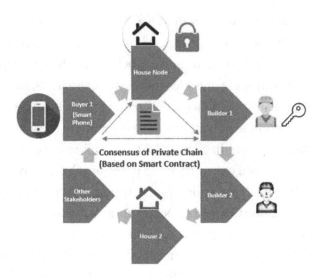

Figure 5-2. *Public and private chain setup for real estate. Upon consensus over the rules of the smart contract on the private ledger, the key access is transferred*

For example, let's observe the following scenario: It is pre-programmed that by March 1, 2020, if the key has not been transferred to the owner due to non-completion of delivery in spite of full payment by buyer, the builder must start paying penalty/rental charges. This condition then gets auto-executed without any discussion. The consensus of the chain adheres to the smart contract, and the transactions are made accordingly in real time. Thus, the penalty is not delayed.

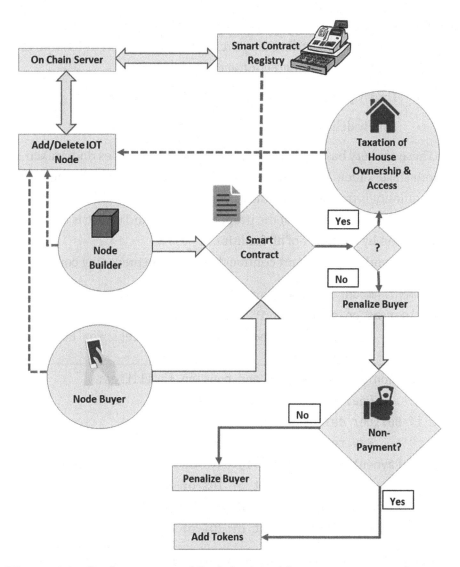

Figure 5-3. *Real estate on a blockchain with smart contracts for stakeholders*

In Figure 5-3, the buyer and the builder are locked into the conditions of the smart contract regarding the purchase of a house. Let us assume the basic conditions that the smart contract may contain:

- Timely payment instalments by buyer to builder

- Timely delivery of housing facilities by builder to buyer

These are very basic but important transaction activities undertaken by both stakeholders in any agreement over a house. Now, when the wallet amount is transferred by the buyer to the builder, the smart contract enables the housing facility of the property. The second clause is the confirmation by the buyer of all facilities.

Pseudo code for the smart contract based on the preceding conditions:

```
If Payment Amount by Buyer by 1st March 2020 == Cost of Property
by Builder as on quote for 1st March 2020:
            Enable House Ownership and Key Access for Buyer on
            1st March 2020.
If Buyer confirms on Access and housing facilities:
            Deal is successfully settled.
Else if Builder delays access and ownership:
            Pay rental cost to Buyer till period of delay
Else If Payment is delayed > 15 days && < 6months by Buyer:
            Penalize interest of 10% of House Cost
Else If Payment is delayed by 6 months by Buyer:
            Penalize interest of 20% of House Cost
```

In another scenario, a tenant stops paying timely rent as promised via traditional paper contract. The owner is harassed by improper communication and delayed payments. Also, on being asked to vacate the premises, tenant fails to do so, making it a legal issue and adding costs, time, and inconvenience to the owner.

If this scenario were to be blockchained, the smart contract would be pre-programmed with the schedule of the payments and what would happen upon the breach of the contract. On mutual agreement via the smart contract on the ledger, indicated by their respective digital signatures, the house node access would transferred to the tenant (enabling physical access) for the said duration of the smart contract. Upon a non-payment on the ledger, the smart contract would self-execute the warning to the tenant to pay within the warning time. If even that probation time is breached, the digital asset key of the house would be auto-transferred to the owner such that the tenant could not re-access. The non-paying tenant would be removed from the private ledger as per the pre-agreed smart contract, barring him from any further transactions (see Figure 5-4).

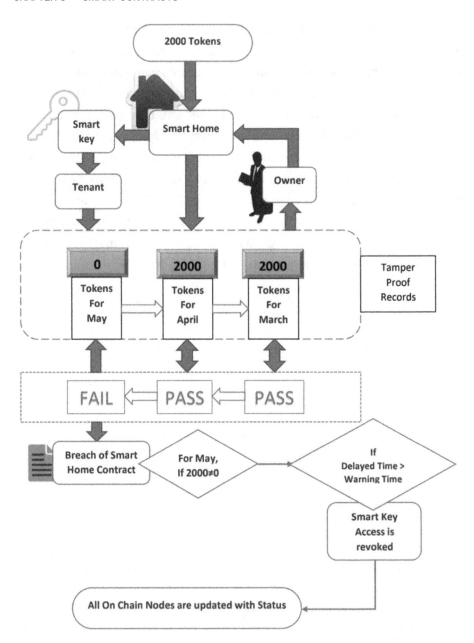

Figure 5-4. *Smart contract execution for a blockchain network between the tenant and owner*

EXERCISE

1. Identify traditional contract use cases and list them.

2. Draw out stakeholders of the identified use cases.

3. Explore the digital assets and transactions involved.

4. Quantify the conditions of movement/status of asset/transactions.

5. Draw flow diagrams of the smart contract construct and execution (similar to Figure 5-4).

6. Based on that, design the pseudo code.

Smart Contract Languages

Once the exercise is completed, the design is to be moved toward development and implementation. For this purpose, let us see the various smart contract languages available for various purposes.

Smart Contract Language	Blockchain Platforms	Features
Solidity	Ethereum, Quorum, Wanchain, Aeternity, Counterparty, Rootstock (RSK), Qtum, Cardano, DFINITY, Soil, Expanse, Ubiq, Ethereum Classic, Monax	• Widely used language • Large number of Integrations with Visual Studio, Remix, Truffle • Multi type safe functions • Maintains the object-oriented structure with inheritances of methods and variables

(*continued*)

Smart Contract Language	Blockchain Platforms	Features
Sophia and Verna	Aeternity	• Functional programming, state, strongly typed, first-class objects, pattern matching, a crowdfunding example
F*	Zen	
RIDEON	Waves	• Enables account control functionalities across multi-chain touchpoints. • Has the ability to implement multi-signature cases, atomic swaps and token freeze limits.
C++, C	EOS, Neo, Neblio, Burst	• Extremely convenient for developer • Tokenizes governance access • A self-sufficient reward model and fee elimination • High-speed parallel processing • Centralization concerns with EOS

(continued)

Smart Contract Language	Blockchain Platforms	Features
C#	Neo, Stratis	• Makes use of the .NET framework • Allows easy integration with enterprise and existing packages in C#
Kotlin	Neo, Corda	• Ease of analysis over state of data • Supports parallel transactions in high-traffic legal entities, including detailed entries • Eliminates mis-ordering of transactions due to the hash functions inbuilt to manage rightly
GoLang	Neo, HyperLedger Fabric, Neblio	• Allows one to build permissioned blockchains with Hyperledger Fabric • Advanced querying capabilities • Active community support

During this survey of all existing smart contracts, there came to light an interesting analysis of Ethereum's largest transactions and the smart contracts for these sets of transactions. The users behind these smart contracts were mainly centralized and decentralized exchanges, ICOs, and token collectors. This was mainly due to the cryptocurrency market which gained high popularity in last couple years. This showcases, smart contracts so far have been used over financial transactions & trade over the Blockchains.

However, the focus of this book being aimed toward the core technology, we shall look into the application side of smart contracts and not tokens—the economics of it. The instability of the crypto-market and this young set of languages makes it highly questionable whether it is worth it for a developer to learn such languages.

Creating Smart Contracts

As we know, smart contracts are programmable contracts that auto-execute based on various activities and transactions, thus fulfilling pre-defined rules. So, for a developer, the design of this logic to create programmable event-based functions is important.

Contracts in the real world often have several loopholes that are then fought over in a legal system. Smart contracts in a blockchain's decentralized world are expected to programmatically cover all cases of a situation for all stakeholders involved. However, it is the developer's design logic that must cover most cases so as to avoid loopholes. Also, several smart contract language compilers may enable these checks to evaluate the Turing completeness. In simpler terms, the compiler needs to check for all cases that is computationally possible to check. This can only be established when the use case is tangible or binary for clear decision-making. Business developers, when considering smart contracts, have to deduce user stories that are tangible so as to enable these features. Refer to the pseudo-code logic in the real estate use case, for example. Thereby smart contracts require the logic to be developed in a way that it covers all cases & covers data driven decisions across the cases.

Smart contracts enable automated execution of decisions based on the data purely. This means that based on the data flowing through the business logic defined in the smart contract, various clauses/actions are triggered. Thereby reducing manual biases of over the data & functions on the pre-defined set of conditions. To be clearer, a delay in payments must cause the addition of interest, which is usually accounted for in large-scale financial transactions or financial institutions. However, there are millions of freelancers who receive delayed payments with no interest. Now, instead of a paper contract, if a freelancer were to engage in business via a smart contract that was programmed to cover the addition of interest for delayed payments from the commissioning company, the effort and delay would be covered aptly. Conversely, if the smart contract were pre-programmed and agreed upon for a timely delivery of the project and the freelancer failed to deliver on time, penalties would be auto-calculated on the ledger, making it a fair programmatic agreement.

Let's look at another use case to further understand the use of smart contracts.

Automobile: Manufacturing, Distribution, Reselling, Servicing

Like homes, cars are enabled smart devices. The readings of the car's performance can be observed in real time and added to the shared ledger of relevant stakeholders. In case of a malfunction, the entire tamper-proof history is clearly available to the servicing nodes of the automobile company. Similarly, the ownership of the vehicle is transferred in real time at the very second of the payment that aligns with the smart contract. Thus, blockchaining the automobile purchase for a first-time buyer from manufacturers through distributors can be performed on-chain, enabling a better user experience for both parties. Now, let's consider a second-hand purchase, where the buyer purchases the vehicle from the seller. In this case, many times, the ownership transfer entails a long procedure with various other stakeholders. If this were to be digitized and validated via a smart contract, the transparency and convenience would be helpful.

For this purpose, we chose Ethereum in the following example. Note that the essence of this practical walkthrough is to help the reader observe the actual implementation. However, the language and the setup may be irrelevant, as it would vary based on the application, time of version, and user requirements of the scenario.

Here is the scenario: There are three types of users on a chain—manufacturer, vendor, and owner (the one who owns the car).

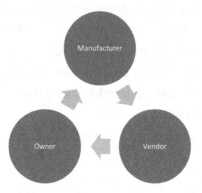

The owner wishes to own a vehicle, books it through the vendor, the vendor orders from the manufacturer, and the vehicle is dispatched after 80 percent of payment has been made. This process traditionally requires the buyer to part ways with the majority of the money first and then have the car dispatched. The transfer of ownership is a longer process compared to the span of time over which the money is paid. With this private chain, the ledger provides a chance for real-time transfer of ownership upon payment of money, with complete transparency between all stakeholders.

To set up the environment for this application, we use the Truffle Suite to develop smart contracts in Ethereum with Azure. Remember: Before choosing the implementation language, one has to design the flow and develop conditions. Upon understanding the nature of the application, one must choose the language and the tools (see Figure 5-5).

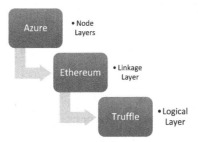

Figure 5-5. *Stack arrangement*

For test purposes, we will start with a small instance to initialize the basic setup on Azure. To set up the environment for this application, we use the Truffle Suite - a development environment, testing framework and asset pipeline for Ethereum. Truffle Suite enables to develop smart contracts with a lot of convenience due to the set of tools inbuilt.

Search the Azure Marketplace for Truffle. One can find several variants on the marketplace. Upon clicking on Truffle, it explains what the suite provides. It enables developers to create virtual accounts over a virtual machine and directly use Truffle tools for smart contracts on Solidity during the pre-setup of an Ethereum blockchain.

Truffle allows you to initialize the VM configuration with the instance name, area zone, and so forth. Choose the desired VM size specs and the region of operation. Select the desired disk specs and proceed to review and create.

Once the steps for the virtual machine are complete, a full set of interconnected resource groups will be ready for use.

Truffle has now provided a VM that is installed with the framework and the ten accounts. The purpose of Truffle here is to provide the basic infrastructure with the Ethereum blockchain nodes and the wallets. See the following:

```
https://docs.google.com/document/d/1GBNlHfLrdOorOKJHedhBSRX43xg
okF9GA7ZIb3ljXO4/edit?usp=sharing
```

These nodes could be local or on Azure instances, based on your configuration. Let us look at the syntactical format of a Solidity smart contract.

We have designed the following smart contract for a manufacturer, for example:

```
pragma solidity ^0.5.4;

contract Manufacturer {
    //Definitions of Users, Objects & States
    address public manufacturer;
    address public vendor;
    address public owner;
    address public car;
    uint public constant price = 4 wei;

    struct car1{
    string cModel;
    uint cRegNo;
    string cLicensePlate;
}

 mapping (address=> uint)public balanceOf;

 car1 carDetail;
//Function Definitions
 function setCar(string memory _cModel, uint _cRegNo, string
 memory _cLicensePlate)public{

    //storing data in struct
    carDetail.cModel= _cModel;
    carDetail.cRegNo= _cRegNo;
    carDetail.cLicensePlate= _cLicensePlate;
}

 function getCar() view public returns(string memory, uint,
 string memory) {
```

```solidity
    return (carDetail.cModel, carDetail.cRegNo, carDetail.
    cLicensePlate);
}

    struct manufacturer1{
    uint mAge;
    string mName;
    string mAddress;
}

mapping(address => manufacturer1) manufacturerDetails;
manufacturer1 manufacturerDetail;

constructor ()public payable

  {
    manufacturer = msg.sender;
    //initialize
    balanceOf[manufacturer] = 0;
}
function setManufacturer(address manufacturer, uint _mAge,
string memory _mName, string memory _mAddress)public{

    //storing data in struct
    manufacturerDetail.mAge= _mAge;
    manufacturerDetail.mName= _mName;
    manufacturerDetail.mAddress= _mAddress;
}

  function getManufacturer(address manufacturer) view public
  returns (uint, string memory, string memory) {
    return (manufacturerDetail.mAge, manufacturerDetail.
    mName, manufacturerDetail.mAddress);
    }
```

```
// State management
enum State1{Created, Locked, Inactive}
State1 public state1;

modifier inState1(State1 _state) {
require(state1 == _state);
_;
}

event PurchaseConfirmed1();
event ItemReceived1();
}
```

The constructs of the smart contract are in three major parts:

1. Definition of Variables – Users, Objects, and States

2. Function Definitions – Read-Write Operations and their accesses

3. Update of state variables based on event triggers

In the preceding code, we have first initialized a contract for a manufacturer, where the definition of variables includes the stakeholders with whom he interacts and objects such as Car that are developed on his end.

The addresses are mapped to the user nodes. The data blocks, such as the status of the manufactured car, are initialized based on the functions. These functions enable the generation of the Car record and its statuses and manufacturer details.

Upon event triggers, the status of the Car object updates are purchased and received according to the contract. Upon these event triggers, the manufacturer's balance may be updated and the car's ownership may be registered.

Note that the syntax of Solidity is not the prime focus of the chapter, but rather the ability to design such smart contracts. The language could be any—C++, Python, Solidity—based on the application, business premise, and developer capacities.

Go ahead and detail out a new use case in food, employment, warranties, or other fields where paper contracts have never helped.

EXERCISE

Think of problems in the current food-supply scenario in your house.

1. Write the challenges you face, such as improper quality, wastage of food, lack of supply, pesticides sprayed, artificially developed food, or an unknown source. Choose one.

2. Identify the stakeholders that handle this food supply for you. E.g., could be your supermarket, online store, or a farm nearby, or the delivery guy, the farmer, the retailer, the wholesaler, etc.

3. Build a block diagram of a block chain representing all these stakeholders.

4. Arrange the linkages of processes involved related to the challenge selected in Step 1. For example, if the challenge is wastage of food, link the inventory node of the house to other fast-consuming houses.

5. Once the chains are linked, decide the type of chain—public, private, or hybrid—and arrange linkages based on it.

6. In a chain, decide on events that require consensus, and the type of consensus.

7. If it is based on a set of pre-defined rules that all stakeholders have to agree upon, implement, or maintain data upon, create a flow diagram of the rules and conditions.

    E.g., if the challenge is quality of food, then link all stakeholders from the farming area, to the distributors, to the delivery to track the conditions of growth, the time of freshness, and have cameras at each node linked on the blockchain (IoT + blockchain). If the delivery node is to maintain the temperature of food at 4 degrees, the sensory nodes could update the blockchain in real time for all stakeholders of this data.

8. When data is added onto the blockchain, the smart contract has to successfully run through the data across the chain to form consensus. If the data (in the preceding example) breaks the rule on the contract, the food is auto-rejected by the buyer, as the supplier couldn't maintain the conditions in the smart contract.

CHAPTER 6

Blockchain Points of Integration

At this stage of the book, we will discover the external and internal interactions of blockchains. Interactions can vary from sourcing of metadata, to onboarding of users, to connecting all the dots of the ecosystem surrounding the blockchain application. This helps us focus on the points of integration that are crucial for a successful seamless workflow that utilizes the benefits of a truly decentralized platform.

Here, the focus is not on the technology itself, but rather on the processes that were in place before the blockchain technology was being considered. While you unfolded different learnings of what a blockchain is in the first half of the book, the second half helps you to visualize its implementation and execution for the challenges around you. Focus on the existing centralized platforms, the people operations, and the offline practices, and revisit each of them closely. Each pain point in the old existing practices will help you identify the right plug (data) point to connect to the blockchain.

© Shilpa Karkeraa 2020
S. Karkeraa, *Unlocking Blockchain on Azure*,
https://doi.org/10.1007/978-1-4842-5043-3_6

We will focus on four important points of integration that make large movements in implementation:

- Data sourcing – Enterprise integration with existing systems

- Onboarding – Compliance and regulatory requirements

- Authorization – Access control and security access

- Automation – Processes for auto-trigger/alerts of smart contracts

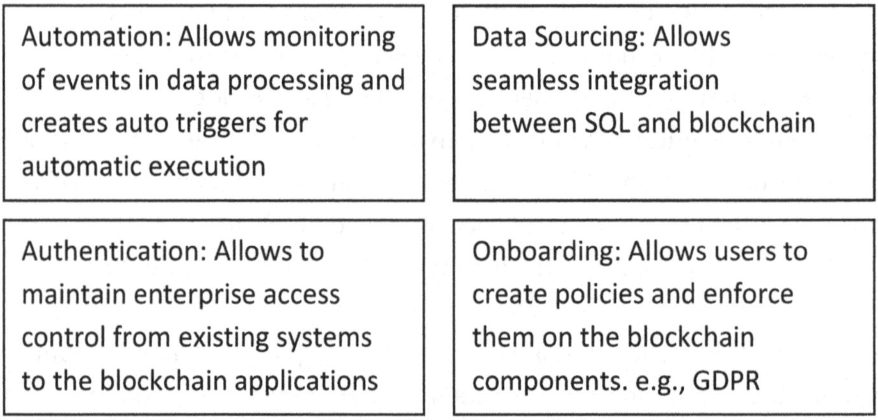

Automation: Allows monitoring of events in data processing and creates auto triggers for automatic execution	Data Sourcing: Allows seamless integration between SQL and blockchain
Authentication: Allows to maintain enterprise access control from existing systems to the blockchain applications	Onboarding: Allows users to create policies and enforce them on the blockchain components. e.g., GDPR

Figure 6-1. *Framework: Point of integration for a blockchain implementation*

Data Sourcing: Enterprise Integration with Existing Systems

One of the prime reasons to learn how to use blockchains with Microsoft Azure is that it brings you the complete infrastructure for this point of integration at an Enterprise level. The Azure Blockchain Workbench allows for a completely agnostic set of options for various types of blockchains and their integration with companies based on existing IT ecosystems and workflows.

With large-scale enterprises becoming more and more data driven, using the correct decentralized practices in digital form has become of utmost importance and drives business decisions. And as organizations across industries would have a varied use case for a block chain application and a very different IT architecture built to cater to its functioning, Microsoft Azure comes in as a bridge that can accommodate both of these challenges. And as organizations get more and more data driven with a lot of aspects of their operations digitizing, the constant tussle of centralizing vs decentralizing shall continue and grow even further. Hence a tool like Microsoft Azure enables organization an easy and sustainable way to decentralize their processes effectively without entirely disturbing existing operations over the Enterprise Tools that were being used before Blockchains.

Consider a 10,000-person organization. The CIO wishes to make business decisions based on company strengths and weaknesses. However, the reporting of this is not very transparent, as there is a hierarchical, non-tangible process by which to derive this data offline. To avoid biases, companies integrate productivity measures in digital form; for example, the number of sales visits, number of converts, value of business, and so forth. These measures existed long before technological tools were introduced. However, with blockchains the process to trace and track these measures has become more transparent and tangible. So, when all actions update on a chain, decision-making can be a closed-loop online activity that measures and drives impact.

With this need to be connected to the stakeholders of the business—be it employees, clients, or suppliers—in tangible, traceable forms that are immutable, decentralized, and secure, blockchains are an obvious Enterprise requirement. The Azure Blockchain Workbench facilitates the smooth integration of Microsoft environments with the various elements of blockchains.

Let us see the variants of data sourcing that require different forms of integration. Data in Enterprises may be of the following types:

- Structured – Databases, CSV files, etc.

- Unstructured – Speech recordings, image scan documents

- B2B – Business-to-business data flow

- B2C – Business and consumer data

- Crowd-sourced – Such as Wikipedia

- Different volumes – Varying scales of data

Based on the type of data and the processes around the data, the mode of integration is selected.

In this chapter, we will focus on the most common form of structured data found in Enterprises across various domains.

Structured Data Sources

Every platform requires metadata to initiate decentralization of any process as well as towards storage of information across the distributed ledger. For instance, before blockchaining the KYC (Know Your Customer) process for a financial institution, one must source the existing data from the centralized software platforms. Most enterprises rely on smooth transitions before investing in any new technology. Based on this common expectation before adoption of Blockchains, Azure SQL Databases, one of the most widely used databases, supports easy integrations for smoother migrations from Legacy Sofwares to the adoption of Blockchains. This integration allows to source the metadata to the platform seamlessly. The flow of structured data could occur in various forms:

- Connectivity to backend systems and existing platforms, such as Microsoft Dynamics 365, which may run ERPs and CRM applications in the organization. In such software, SQL servers are used, which can be smoothly integrated with the blockchains for data-sourcing purposes (Figure 6-2).

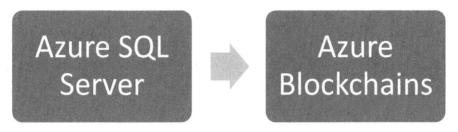

Figure 6-2. *Data sourcing from Azure SQL Database servers to Azure blockchains*

- Certain activities may be on the chain and certain are allowed to be off chain. When the impact of blockchains does not affect the storage of data for reporting or display purposes (non-audit related), storage onto SQL can easily be off-loaded (Figure 6-3).

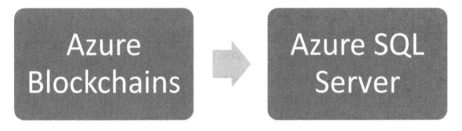

Figure 6-3. *Delivery of data from distributed ledgers to off-chain databases, such as SQL servers on Azure*

- Bi-directional flow of data based on different purposes and triggers. Blockchains may store on SQL servers non-trivial data that could be used for intermediate reporting and analytics.

- SQL servers may invoke different logic apps and event triggers in the Azure Blockchain Workbench whenever the threshold of data limiters is crossed, as defined in the smart contracts or consensus algorithms (Figure 6-4).

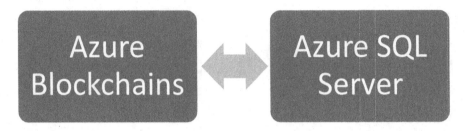

Figure 6-4. *Shared set of action items in terms of data distribution for different purposes*

Connectivity and Definition of SQL Integrations with Blockchains

There are two steps in this process:

1. Establishing connectivity. The SQL Server Management Studio provides a preview of the SQL storage in the Blockchain Workbench. Before defining the database schema, you can see the changes in data flow. The basic step of integration is to set up the right set of IP addresses for the blockchain nodes and the SQL server. Then you must enable the Read-Write settings based on the directional flow of data.

2. Defining database views, application views, application role views such as buyers and sellers, user allocation to the application user, and the connection status of the application user.

Other ERP integrations involving PowerBI, SAP, and Excel could also be sourced to fit the blockchain ecosystems.

Azure Cosmos DB Integrations with Blockchains

Azure Cosmos DB is a globally distributed, multi-model database service for any scale. This NoSQL database provides multi-master nodes with connectivity across the globe while transparently maintaining replicas throughout. However, this is not to be confused with blockchains. Azure Cosmos DB appropriately aligns and integrates aspects of shared distributed ledgers with blockchains.

When you require an immutable, append-only ledger and are dealing with multiple parties in a trustless network with known permissioned stakeholdership, you need a combination of permissioned blockchains with Cosmos DB to maintain the distributed storage and traceability.

In other cases, where consensus is not a prime requirement, Cosmos DB may suffice without the blockchains. Such cases include those where distribution is maintained and aspects such as encryptions can be implemented on top of the arrangement. One of the Unique Selling Proposition (USP)/key differentiators of considering Azure Cosmos DB is its openness to integration with other technologies, while at the same time allowing decentralization from its foundation, along with other aspects of blockchains.

Platforms that wish to decentralize could easily transition from SQL, MongoDB, Gremlin Graph, Cassandra, Tables, and CSVs to Azure's Cosmos DB on a large global scale.

Let's understand a use case for Azure Cosmos DB with blockchains and then get into the technical details.

Let's understand the use case by Microsoft over the XBOX Game Publishers' Royalties that are accessible over the Azure Blockchain Services. This example, showcases the transparency facilitated in terms of tracing royalties from a credible source. Game publishers can access royalty statements through this assembly of technology. The process involved is a mix of on-chain tracing, off-chain visualizations & immutable audit of processes. Thereby Azure Cosmos DB enables the distributed storage of the royalties across the globe whereas the Blockchain Service maintains the states of all processes maintaining credibility of the information stored. The Blockchain Service also enables the automation of rules over the royalties in the form of Smart Contracts.

Let's break down the implementation to better understand the process flow.

1. Metadata is sourced from off-chain storage, such as Azure Cosmos DB, SQL, or MongoDB.

2. Blockchain nodes are initialized with the required information and the purpose of consensus, if defined.

3. Further elements, such as event triggers, allow serverless code to be driven on-chain with alerts and triggers.

Here are the steps for integration:

1. Reshape data schema to Azure Cosmos DB from SQL centralized forms.

2. Restructure data structures to key value, column family, documents, and graphs.

3. Global distribution

4. Create a multi-master replication protocol based on validation only or a form of consensus.

5. Check geographical limitations and policies.

6. Identify the levels of trust and permissions required for the processes.

7. Stack elements relevant to the processes.

These steps are applicable when the distributed ledgers of data require the blockchain aspects of connected validations and triggers of smart contracts. One needs to identify the right confluence of integration for a seamless experience.

For example, enterprises that maintain large-scale data jobs on Apache Spark can seamlessly connect to Cosmos DB for the append-only transparent ledger. Further, if the data jobs require a closed-loop consensus, Azure Blockchain Workbench enables it. See: `https://docs.microsoft.com/en-us/azure/cosmos-db/spark-connector`.

Similar integrations can be established for IoT hub networks as well as SharePoint systems with blockchains.

Onboarding: Compliance and Regulatory Requirements

Once the sourcing of data is identified, data is sorted, structured, and stored appropriately. The classification of data for private and public blockchains as well as for on-chain and off-chain activities is crucial. Such classification is linked to the policies that establish protection rights and regulations with which every business must comply.

At the same time, the process by which the data is handled is crucial, along with the state of the data, when we talk about blockchains. For instance, a normal registration of a centralized online platform merely requires an email and password set up, with some more details. However, the process of storing the password and email is unknown to the end user. There may be unsecured platforms that store passwords in plain-text and may leak out values that could be used on secured platforms as well. Thus, onboarding a user onto a blockchain differs from such common practices.

Onboarding starts with the machine addresses, private and public keys, and the validation of other nodes, depending on the type and purpose of the blockchain.

Therefore, the second touchpoint of consideration is how this sourcing of data is seamlessly onboarded to blockchains. This onboarding may be at the start of the blockchain setup, or during intervals, or during ongoing operations, or during any number of event triggers.

However, how it is done is highly crucial to keeping the sensitivity of the data and the credibility of its state in mind. As this integration touchpoint is quite vulnerable to attack, the following aspects have to be scoped out:

- Cybersecurity

- Compliance

- Regulations

- Geographic policies (e.g., Europe)

  - GDPR

  - PSD2 and e-Privacy

- Industrial domain policies

  - Maritime

  - Manufacturing

  - Medical

This integration touchpoint does not have direct tools to implement; it is more of a design consideration for the integration of processes related to onboarding. This varies highly based on the application, location, and domain of the blockchain platform.

GDPR Considerations for Blockchains

The **General Data Protection Regulation** (EU) 2016/679 (**GDPR**) is a regulation in EU law that covers data protection and privacy for all individual citizens of the European Union (EU) and the European Economic Area (EEA). It also addresses the transfer of personal data outside the EU and EEA areas. The GDPR aims primarily to give control to individuals over their personal data and to simplify the regulatory environment for international business by unifying the regulations within the EU.

This consists of three main aspects.

Definition of Purpose and Consent

While onboarding users, the definition of purpose must be clearly conveyed. Along with this, the rightful consents to use the data must be clearly described. This European policy has ensured such practices on a centralized platform. How does this apply to blockchains? The answer is in the smart contract triggers, which may comply and check in case of any deviation. For example, if a user has not provided consent, the blockchain platform must clearly convey and commit to the bylaws defined in the foundation of that blockchain.

Subject Access Request (SAR)

Upon the request of a user, SAR allows the retrieval of all personal information for that user from the platform. On an immutable ledger facilitated by blockchains, the complete history of data is traceable yet secure as the ability to access this data resides purely with the user.

Failure to comply with this provision may penalize the company with a fine of up to 20 million GBP or 4 percent of global turnover, whichever is higher. Such clauses may auto-trigger when such bylaws are broken. But the question here is, why would companies ever program a blockchain to become such non-profitable systems? The answer to this is that it enables the users to also have a beneficial contract during onboarding. The governance mechanism must require both stakeholders - the organizations & the users to comply with the regulations put forth in the smart contract mutually. It gives the user an avenue to put forth his terms. It may involve penalties or refunds based on the conditions agreed by both parties as a part of consensus. Since the user here is not a mere subscriber, this peer-to-peer relationship is master to master, and so the clauses must be balanced.

Data Breach Notification

The user must be notified if the platform faces a security breach so that suitable actions can be taken by the user. This also can be a part of a smart contract during onboarding.

Based on these three aspects, the Azure Compliance Manager extends an array of tools to be utilized for any policy defined over the cloud components and enforced throughout. This does not mean it comes embedded with the Azure Blockchain suite, but since the architecture lies in the same environment, it is easier to integrate them for their specific purposes.

More here: `https://azure.microsoft.com/en-in/overview/trusted-cloud/compliance/`.

Azure's Compliance Manager offers various tools for various purposes. It covers an array of global policies and regulations across countries, industries, and timelines.

Azure Blueprints

Azure Blueprints allows businesses to utilize templates that are pre-defined as per policies and regulations, such as ISO, GDPR, etc., or to make custom templates for the entire organization to follow while building independent applications or company-wide applications. (This is currently a free service offered by Azure, allowing one to adhere to international policies, but it is not known how long they will keep it that way.)

When building international blockchains with users across different industries and countries, these templates must be considered to avoid national conflicts over data privacy and protection rights.

Azure Policy

Here, independent policies are defined. As we saw, Blueprints provides a template/framework for policies and security rules. The policy definition takes place in this tool. The blockchain policies for nodes and transactions can be stored here while designing universal policies.

Azure Security Center

When one activates the Security Center on Azure, a monitoring agent is actively deployed over the virtual machine components. It actively checks for threats and attacks. Similar to the security checks for SQL injections, brute-force attacks, and so forth in centralized systems, blockchain nodes have to be actively monitored for the same.

In case, in a trustless permissionless network, there are collusions observed in the patterns of fraudulent validations, the Security Center could trigger policies to avoid such attacks and safeguard the on-chain activities (Figure 6-5).

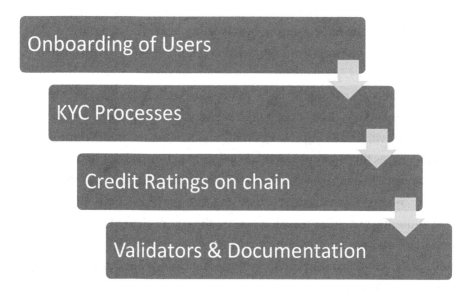

Figure 6-5. *Security processes*

EXERCISE

Refer to the preceding process flow and identify the right integration
components for this flow in an insurance company.

Authorization: Access Control and Security Access

Most enterprises enforce access control for various roles and activities.
Based on the login credentials and metadata from the preceding stages,
the proper access control is selected and functionalities are catered. Now,
in case of an attack, if the lowest authority becomes vulnerable, the entire
hierarchy of control will fall. Therefore, considering the ongoing practices
of access control, it is highly crucial to embed the existing processes of
access control onto the blockchain.

Azure Active Directory is widely used to maintain access control over
all applications based on a common protocol. This component requires
integration with the decentralized blockchain platform. The entity of
access control is mapped from the existing record of users to the hashed
machine addresses.

Another aspect of security is the **Azure Key Vault**, where the user
stores and maintains their set of public keys and backs up the private keys
if desired. However, storing keys centrally again defies the initial purpose of
blockchains, as the key could be made vulnerable to attacks or leaks, making
it less secure. The main reason to use the Azure Key Vault is to seamlessly
integrate the existing security mechanisms with the blockchain activities.

Another form of authorization is the validator nodes, which are
dependent on human intervention to approve new peers. There could be
nodes assigned to forming consensus to issue CA certificates authorizing a
new user on the chain.

Lastly, smart contracts may enforce a checklist of pre-requisites for the user, perhaps a minimum set of documents or a biometric scan and iris scan, to gain authorization.

The smart contract integration for such an application must consist of the following:

- Right to access – It should allow users to understand how the contract is designed.

- Restricted programming – It should eliminate vague definitions in code.

- Informed triggers and alerts – It should activate conditional activities as defined.

- Forgotten state or deletion actions – It should manage states of data on rollbacks and deletion requests.

Automation: Processes for Auto-trigger/Alerts of Smart Contracts

Since the onset of the digital era, most businesses have transitioned online, including bringing their data online. However, there are still large-scale companies relying on off-chain practices due to a failure to integrate with modern systems.

This is exactly where automation by smart contracts can facilitate faster transactions. Smart contracts not only digitizes contract data but also digitizes the states/ processes that are involved in transferring the data.

This integration can be achieved as follows:

- REST APIs

- Azure event triggers

- Azure's logic apps to service bus

- Workbench modifications in consensus rule

Let us examine a medical transport scenario where smart contracts are to be integrated.

Consider organ transplants, which require the organ to quite literally be transacted transparently in a secure environment from the donor to the patient. Here, the data and the process around this transaction are highly sensitive. There are several state flows to be considered:

- Organ is safely transported in the right environment.

- Organ is tampered with at the source.

- Organ transport had a mishap and temperature was not maintained.

- Organ was infected during delivery at destination.

The state flow of the organ is highly crucial for the suitable outcome of the transplant. If the donor, the doctor extracting the organ, the transport conditions (via IoT), and the delivery check on the recipient side are all on a blockchain bound with a smart contract clause for a healthy organ for a successful transplant, and if any node supplies data that has tampered with the state of the organ and its environment variables, then the recipient can transparently avoid a faulty transaction. These auto-triggers and alerts can be on the chain through the Azure event trigger at the very moment the any of the conditions (defined in the smart contract) for a healthy organ fails the contract.

For example, if the cooling system during transfer were to fail, the event trigger would invoke the Azure logic app to update the state to indicate an unsuccessful transfer. This provides a safe, transparent, clause-driven ecosystem with blockchains and the smart contract.

Complete Picture

The key to a successful working ecosystem is design (Figure 6-6). Having the right set of components aligned ensures each of the components stands up to the expectations of its functionality and at the same time maintains the conjunction of processes that were already in practice. While bringing decentralization and automation through blockchain and smart contracts to organizations that have long been run in a particular way, such changes are difficult and often break into offline processes, leading to discrepancies and opaque layers of clarity.

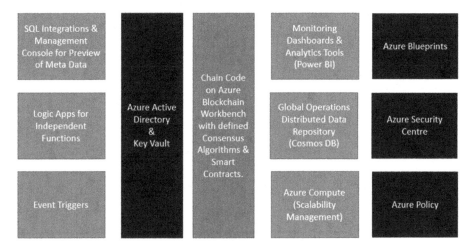

Figure 6-6. *Azure components for seamless integration*

Design considerations and awareness of what can be seamlessly integrated are highly crucial. This chapter has aimed to cover those thoughts and considerations in terms of the availability in the Microsoft Azure ecosystem of the components around the Azure blockchain, as shown in the Figure 6-5.

These independent Azure Components are well tested and compliant for the services described above and are widely used across enterprises. Thereby Blockchains must not be seen as a stand alone system during its adoption. It is recommended to plan integration of existing systems with Blockchains to run operations seamlessly.

Thus with this, identify the touchpoints and Azure services that suit the purposes of your blockchain and the processes around it.

CHAPTER 7

Technological Tools

This chapter will decode the array of tools that enable designing, constructing, and operating various aspects of blockchains in a decentralized application. We shall walk through how these tools can be chained on-cloud and off-cloud with Microsoft Azure's cloud services.

The blockchain solution lifecycle has three stages of development:

1. Business requirements and causes of decentralization

2. Solution architecture with respect to operations

3. Developer's version of technical component breakdown

We will use the top-down approach toward identifying tools for blockchain implementations.

Business Requirements and Causes of Decentralization

Business developers identify the pain points in an existing business, workflow, or operations. For any technology to be implemented, its ability to be effective in helping the business achieve desired outcomes is extremely important. Thus, before any technology decision is made, carving out the business requirements is of utmost importance. Fill in the CAUSE Matrix in Table 7-1 to understand the selection of blockchain types required for your business application.

© Shilpa Karkeraa 2020
S. Karkeraa, *Unlocking Blockchain on Azure*,
https://doi.org/10.1007/978-1-4842-5043-3_7

Table 7-1. CAUSE Matrix for Business Developers to Shape the Blockchain Use Case

C Collaborative workflow?	A Assets digitized?	U Unknown contributors?	S Storage of State?	E Encryption Crucial?	Blockchain Required?	Type of Blockchain?
Is the workflow designed to be collaborative?	Can the asset be digitized or not?	Are the contributors known or unknown?	Should the history of states be recorder?	Is encryption crucial or not?		
Yes	Yes	Yes	Yes	Yes	Yes	Public blockchain
Yes	Yes	No	Yes	Yes	Yes	Private blockchain
Yes	Yes	Both (Access Control)	Yes	Yes	Yes	Hybrid blockchain
No	Yes	Yes	No	Yes	No	Any other centralized platforms
Yes	No	Yes	Yes	No	No	Any other centralized platforms

CAUSE Matrix helps businesses in designing the blockchain solutions. It is a 5 factor questionnaire that business strategists must fill in to derive whether Blockchain is required or not and further identify the type of Blockchain suitable for it.

It is a way to evaluate if blockchains are required in your business application.

Based on the result of the matrix, you can identify if the business scenario really requires blockchains or not.

Mark "yes" for "collaborative workflow" when the entire flow of operations needs to be linked digitally by multiple users. For example, consider a business use case where a team of 50 HR workers runs personnel operations across a Fortune 500 company that has 50,000 employees. The company wishes to bind all activities together, connecting various aspects of personnel operations. This collaborative workflow can be on chain, thereby marking it as "Yes."

For "assets digitized," the entity on record is employees that may be digitized based on the data records. If assets are not digital, one has to find a way to connect the physical asset to a digital one. For example, house-key access can be done through a smartphone or a biometric key that can be used as a data asset on the ledger.

"Unknown contributors" is to evaluate if the stakeholders/users of the business process are end customers who are unknown and exploratory or known entities such as employees, business partners, or service providers. Based on that, public or private blockchains or both, forming hybrid blockchains, are used.

"Storage of state" is to recognize if the data being recorded is required to store each state or just the last state. Referring to our example, if the HR worker needs to know the entire lifecycle of an employee, all state records are crucial, and therefore using a blockchain is legit as it provides a tamperproof record of all states of an employee. Conversely, in a case where only the last case matters, a blockchain may not be needed. A simple ERP/CRM could be used.

Lastly, the factor for encryption helps to decide if end-to-end encryption is required. In a large organization, certain network information needs to be kept internal and confidential, and thus a private ledger could be used that encrypts valuable information between the relevant stakeholders only. In our example, data points such as salary need to be end-to-end encrypted between the employee and the HR department. The storage of such data is encrypted and distributed on-chain, making it difficult for a hacker to target one server to break out the information.

Based on the outcome of the CAUSE matrix, refer to various examples of blockchains in Table 7-2. The specific alignment of your use case to the blockchain can be further deduced in the second matrix in the solution architect's phase of choice.

Table 7-2. *Technology Platforms for Blockchain with Public, Private, and Hybrid*

Public Blockchains	Private Blockchains	Hybrid Blockchains
• Hedera Hashgraph	• Hyperledger	• DragonChain
• Bitcoin	• Quorum	• EWF
• Ethereum	• Bankchain	• B3i
• Litecoin	• MONAX	• R3 Corda
• Monero	• MultiChain	
• MeWe		
• Choon		
• MINDS		

Business developers have to identify the area of operation that requires decentralization based on the CAUSE factors so as to decide on the type of blockchain.

Businesses that operate toward expanding services on a decentralized ledger to consumers who may be unknown end users who require no permission to join the ledger opt for a public blockchain. Businesses that operate in a B2B environment or internal to the company may utilize a private blockchain, where permission is crucial for controlled parameters.

In the case of a marketplace business case, for instance, a combination of private and public blockchain networks is required, forming hybrid blockchains. Certain information, such as retail goods listings and service listings, may be put on the public blockchain, and the users can anonymously view the data on the public blockchain ledger. However, when there is a transaction between a buyer and a seller, a private blockchain network can be formed, and the transactions may operate based on the consensus principle of the chain.

Business developers seek enterprise technology tools for deployments, especially to receive long-term support, scalability, skill availability, training, and so forth (Figure 7-1). Azure provides a wide range of enterprise support for its blockchain elements along with its other cloud services. This improves the integration capacity of the existing Microsoft framework so it can be on-cloud and on-chain wherever required.

Figure 7-1. *Key tools for blockchains with Azure*

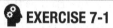 **EXERCISE 7-1**

As a business developer, identify a business case that truly requires a blockchain. Run the use case through the CAUSE matrix and confirm suitability. Break down the use case into specific aspects, such as:

1. Storage

2. Process

3. Access control

4. Contracts

5. Tokens

Write user story across each aspect based on the business use case.

This exercise further provides solution architects with tools to decide the specifics of the blockchain platform.

Solution Architecture with Respect to Operations

After selecting from among public, private, or hybrid blockchains, one has to check the factors laid out by the solution architect's questionnaire in order to build the platform. Walk through every cell in Table 7-2 and review your business use case's situation with respect to the attribute.

Table 7-3. *21 Questions for Business and Developer-based Decision for a Solution Architect*

Scalability	Use case	Community	Skill availability	Adaptability	Security	Regulatory risk
	dependent on cryptocurrency/ any kind of quantification	support/ enterprise support				
1	2	3	4	5	6	7
High Performance Millisecond transactions	Rewarded on-chain or off-chain	Industry-specific developments	Control functionality intra-firm inter-firm consensus	Integrations with existing systems or standalone	Governance	Trust/trustless Permissioned/ permission less Open/close networks
8	9	10	11	12	13	14
Who maintains integrity? Selected member or all	Contractual relationship of users with business logic	Identity/KYC crucial? Private transactions?	Cost optimizations in a multi-stakeholder process?	Improve discoverability and self-triggered automation?	Custom requirements/ DIY Solutions/ BAAS/ Development platforms	Domain knowledge to design decentralization
15	16	17	18	19	20	21

165

Use Case: Sharing Medical Health Records of Patients Across Hospitals

In cases of medical treatment, it has been observed that it is not always the same doctor or hospital treating a patient over a period of time. This may happen due to the patient relocating to a different place, a referral from the current hospital to another hospital, being in an unfortunate incident in some other city, or simply because the patient does not like the approach of the doctor. In such cases, it becomes important to have the complete medical history of the patient shared with the new hospital/doctor in order to maintain continuity of care and appropriate understanding of the patient's illness and past treatments.

As medical records are highly personal and confidential documents, it is important to have the data available in a format that is secured, immutable, and available only to the right users. This creates a window to explore the feasibility of solving this problem using a blockchain.

Exploring further, we observe that based on the CAUSE matrix, the use of a blockchain is surely suitable, as it has the following:

- Multiple contributors and collaborators

- Health records are assets

- Both types of contributors

    - Known (certified professionals, doctors, and hospitals)

    - Unknown (end users, patients, customers)

- Every state of the health record is crucial

- This immutable data has to be fully end-to-end encrypted on-chain for full anonymity and privacy.

Now, let's identify the solution architect's questionnaire:

Scalability	Use Case Dependent on Cryptocurrency/ Any Kind of Quantification	Community Support / Enterprise Support	Skill Availability	Adaptability	Security	Regulatory Risk
Number of patient records is large. Concurrency of active patient care is also high.	Not yet, medical health index could be used for insurance purposes	Enterprise support used by hospitals	No, experts with the confluence of medical and technology are rare	Yes, adaptable for varied demographics, geographies, situations	Requires high security and data privacy	Compliance with medical regulations is a must.
1	2	3	4	5	6	7

(continued)

167

#	Question/Factor	Response
8	High-performance millisecond transactions	Yes
9	Rewarded on-chain or off-chain	Can be both
10	Industry-specific developments	No
11	Control functionality intra-firm or inter-firm consensus	Inter-firm
12	Integrations with existing systems or standalone	Yes
13	Governance	Yes
14	Trust/trustless Permissioned/permissionless Open/closed networks	Trustless permissioned/closed networks
15	Who maintains integrity?	Selected member
16	Contractual relationship of users with business logic	Contractual relationship
17	Identity/KYC crucial? Private transactions?	Identity/KYC Crucial
18	Cost optimizations in a multi-stakeholder process?	Yes
19	Improve discoverability and self-triggered automation?	Yes
20	Custom requirements/ DIY solutions/ BAAS/ development platforms	Custom requirements
21	Domain knowledge to design decentralization	Yes

GHOSTTT Protocol

Once the business team defines the vision of the Blockchain platform & specifies the type of the blockchain through the CAUSE Matrix, solution architects have to identify deeper components of design that bridge business & technology.

Thereby we coined the GHOSTTT protocol that enables solution architects to factor design touchpoints for Blockchains as follows:

- **Governance** required? Single-handedly, selective authority, all nodes contribute to governance, or consensus based on smart contract rules?

- **High-speed** transactions and concurrency? Hybrid chains of private ledgers in a smaller network mesh.

- **Open**/closed, permissioned or permissionless?

- Large-scale data **Storage** of states – Custom solutions for developing consensus across distributed servers where data is stored with copies across the private chains based on the platform mechanism.

- **Storage** on-chain distributed and copied? Does the state of transactions interact based on events on chain?

- **Tokens** required? Existing scoring mechanism? Reward program? Shortcomings? Auto-calibration of value required?

- **Transactions** interact with known participants – distributed ledgers, Ripple, Corda

- **Trusted** networks or trustless?

The solution architect's responsibility here is to identify the right set of tools that aligns with the business as well as the developer skill set available. The GHOSTTT protocol translates the business demands

169

for technology decisions. After the CAUSE matrix is clarified, one has to deduce the specifics based on the GHOSSTTT protocol.

Let's consider the GHOSSTTT protocol for the use case of sharing medical health records of patients across hospitals.

Governance

Governance in this growing digital era has brought out new challenges that may have not been factored earlier in ecosystems, enterprises & platforms. With the need to cover fair practices while storing, referring & transacting on digital platforms, governance needs to evolve. With Blockchains, Decentralized Autonomous organizations (DAO) regulation systems are introduced. This system enables the stakeholders participating to be governed by a common set of pre-defined rules agreed by all. No action out of these rules are allowed in a DAO based system. So while designing Blockchains, one must factor if any such regulatory measures have to be defined in the smart contracts to enable Autonomous Functions unbiased by any party on chain. Even unbiased to the party initiating or hosting the Blockchain.

In the medical use case explained earlier, the conditions for a healthy organ form a part of governance to maintain integrity of the process, unbiased to the medical institution provisioning the service. This is the main differentiator from a mere website hosted by the medical institution which can be manipulated, however, the records on a DAO based Blockchain cannot be tampered, maintaining the governance as desired.

High-Speed Transactions and Concurrency

Azure CosmosDB provides a low-latency, high-availability and globally distributed, multi-model database to enable such transactions as well as to run concurrent transactions in consortium networks. Similar NoSQL databases can be selected for this factor.

Medical records are generated at every instant in various parts of the world and are indexed several times from the ledger for various stakeholders. Therefore, the low latency is a crucial factor for a decentralized ledger.

Open or Closed, Permissioned or Permissionless

For health care, a lot of information is distributed openly to the stakeholders in terms of medical services, policies, and so forth. However, access to confidential information such as medical records is required to be permissioned. Therefore, the chain could be an open permissioned ledger.

For example, Azure Marketplace provides Quorum, which maintains privacy for transactions and contracts by separating the public and private data over separate networks, thus maintaining the privacy for private data and the transparency for public data.

Storage

In a distributed ledger for a blockchain platform, there are two aspects: one is the decentralized storage of state of the chain nodes, and the second is the storage of data. At this stage, one has to decide if the application is across an intranet, internet, or a shared disk with virtual node clusters.

Considering the sharing of medical records and the choice of Quorum in the preceding points, Quorum ensures the privacy of transactions and the state of transactions and not the data storage itself. Therefore, the storage of states is encrypted and can be stored in Azure's Blob or CosmosDB or any other storage. However, for an application where the storage of data is more crucial than the transaction itself, tools such as BigChainDB, which extends to distributed storage of data, may be considered. If files are to be encrypted as is, IPFS can be considered. In cases where medical records are to be stored and transacted/shared securely, one can design Quorum to be integrated with IPFS for Azure cloud components to make sharing medical records truly safe and the storage equally vaulted across the globe.

Tokens, Transactions, and Trust

Medical records being a highly sensitive document with respect to patient health, the credibility of the source of the medical records is highly crucial. Therefore, the DAO selected in the first stage of governance establishes the trust of an unbiased network. Having the voting mechanism on-chain for authorization boards doing the certifying makes the record more trustworthy. Transactions here may be sharing records, buying medical tests and reports, or purchasing general anonymized public data within the regulations of the chain. Here, the solution architect has to design the consortium chain, which could be a public chain within a country, region, or area, or private chains of medical doctors and patients, or private chains of enterprises and the medical records of their employees, or private networks of insurance companies and customers. The wiring of transaction networks is to be decided at this stage. Once this is designed, based on the business requirements, quantification of on-chain actions can be made. So, first decide if tokenization is required in your business use case; for example, credit ratings of a hospital/surgeon/pathologist. Credit ratings of customers for health insurance companies and so on can be incentivized on-chain with the token-economics agreed to on-chain. However, for simply maintaining a digital vault on the ledger, no tokenization is required.

EXERCISE 7-2. BASED ON THE BUSINESS CASE IN EXERCISE 7-1, ANSWER THE OUTCOMES OF GHOSSTTT PROTOCOL FOR YOUR USE CASE

When points of governance, high speed, and open networks are clear, start surveying the technology tools suitable for the pain points. In many cases, a certain combination of tools may not be readily present. That's where the solution architect has to decide to either develop from scratch, choose an existing blockchain solution, or pick an enterprise structure of cloud-based components such as Azure for the blockchain network.

After this exercise, walk through the "21 Questions for Business- and Developer-based Decisions for a Solution Architect" table. Finalize the technology stack and architecture in iteration with Sections 1 and 3.

Application of GHOSTTT Protocol

The next step is to stack up the layers of the GHOSTTT protocol into a block diagram to formulate the overall process flow and architecture. For example let's understand the architecture laid by the Azure Blockchain Workbench, as shown in Figure 7-2.

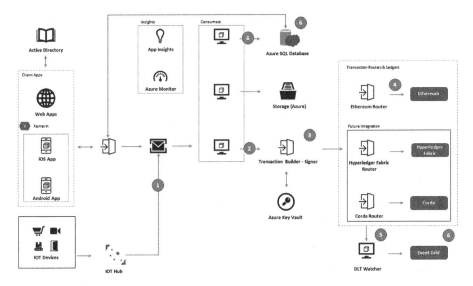

Figure 7-2. *Components of Azure*

Combining the answers from the GHOSTTT protocol and the 21-question matrix, the solution architect has to decide on either a top-to-bottom approach (customer first to backend infrastructure) or a bottom-to-top approach (backend infrastructure to customer interface). With an ecosystem such as Azure, all components of a blockchain application are covered.

For example in Figure 7-2, a top-to-bottom approach consists of the following:

- User authentication (Cell No. 17) – Azure Active Directory

- Application interface (Cell No. 20) – Xamarin apps and IoT edge devices with IoT Hub

- Data communication channels (Cell no. 12) – REST-based gateway service API, message brokers, service bus

- Consumers such as DLT (on-chain), database (off-chain), and hash storage (encrypted) consumers

- Insights – Azure Monitor and analytics

- Transaction builder and signer – Azure Key Vault

- Transaction routers and ledgers

- DLT watcher and event grid

These tools are highly reliable when customers are located across geographical areas with the means to connect over a reliable internet connect, as well as for an organization that is looking for an enterprise infrastructure of cloud components to drive the blockchain.

Revisiting the CAUSE matrix, why is a blockchain required in such a case, and not a centralized hosted system?

Because for hosting parties that develop and host such platforms, encryption is usually at the mercy of the developers or under the governance of the company hosting such a service. Therefore, such platforms have low credibility in terms of public trust on a large scale. In a blockchain network, the encryption is distributed across a network, making it difficult to decrypt by any random attacker. Also, in a blockchain mode of governance, where the process runs on a decentralized, autonomous system that can be seen as a set of pre-defined, agreed-upon rules set in a smart contract, replacing the rules ad hoc is not allowed until all members agree and validate the change of rule or until consensus is achieved on the change.

So far, we have gotten a bird's eye view of the architecture used to form a decentralized blockchain application, along with the components that form the ledger and the support components that drive the application. Further drill-downs inside the blockchain architectures of Ethereum, Hyperledger, and so forth can be found in the next chapter.

The following is a list of top-to-bottom functional components for a decentralized application:

- Front-end components
  - Applications
  - Block explorers
  - Monitoring systems (watchers, event trigger alerts)
  - Smart contract tools
    - Definitions with Solidity and other smart contract languages
    - Auto-validators, enforcers of the contract
  - Pre-defined standards and governance
    - for tokens
    - for identity
    - for actions
- Tooling components
  - Active Directory
  - Wallets
  - Vaults
  - Data Warehouse integrations
  - Integration plugins
    - Json RPC
    - Inter-Chains
    - Oracles

- Privacy and scaling components

  - Encryption

  - Hashing

  - Computing

  - Concurrency of service buses

- Core blockchain components

  - Network configuration

  - On-chain and off-chain states and storage

  - Execution of smart contracts

  - Consensus

    - for private networks

    - for public networks

- Network protocols

  - Devp2p

  - Enterprise P2p

  - RLPx wire

  - Libp2p

Azure Stack

Once the mechanisms and the component structure are defined for the use case at hand, Design Architecture can be allocated to the development teams based on the type of component, function, and role. Note that once the solution architect finalizes the stack with the GHOSSTTT protocol,

21-question matrix, and the component list, curating the actual execution of true decentralization is of utmost importance. Proceeding further, we must raise the following questions to improve the stack:

- How is this credibility established?

- How is the true decentralization validated?

- How is governance tested and enforced?

Having an enterprise ecosystem where all third parties also align with the definitions of components meant for true decentralization, trust, and peer-to-peer networks is crucial.

Azure Stack provides a single-click deployment option for the Ethereum network wherein each member can contribute to the network. The contributing member on-chain may run a set of nodes that interact/transact with the other mining nodes on the chain. Azure lets one decide the chain topology using network virtual appliance and connection resources for single- or multi-member Ethereum consortium networks.

In an enterprise setup that works B2B (for example, NBFCs working with DSAs for loan disbursals or insurance companies working with insurance agencies), there are multiple companies working with on another. The technical implementation of this business setup requires nodes of the Blockchain communicate across different Azure accounts that belong to different businesses.

In a setup where the processes are to be decentralized within an organization, amongst different departments/employees of the same organization, the nodes of the Blockchain will be a part of the same organization subscription for Azure (cell nos. 11 and 16 of the 21-question set).

In a multi-node Azure Stack, there are the following template components:

- Standalone and consortium leader deployment (also exists in single-node) – the initiator

- Joining consortium member deployment – the joining members

- Connecting other members with the initiator/genesis node

Azure provides the template for both components/members with a deployment option to run the template. For details on executing the template, see the following: `https://docs.microsoft.com/en-us/azure-stack/user/azure-stack-ethereum#standalone-and-consortium-leader-deployment`.

As a solution architect, one has to identify the existing templates Azure provides in its marketplace with respect to the business case, GHOSTTT protocol, and 21-question matrix.

Azure provides the following Ethereum alternatives.

Quorum: EEA Single-Member Blockchain

Quorum is an open source, permissioned implementation of Ethereum that focuses on securely processing transactions and restricts access based on the permission status of control (see Figure 7-4). Figure 7-3 highlights the essential components that power a QuorumChain. Observing the transactions of Ethereum on Quorum, we see how all of these components come alive to interact with each other in Figure 7-4.

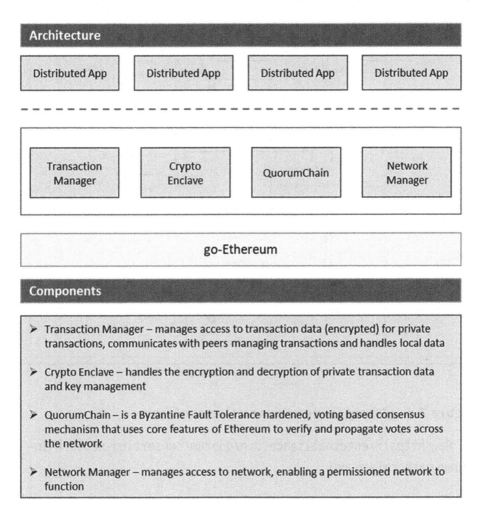

Figure 7-3. *Architecture of a QuorumChain*

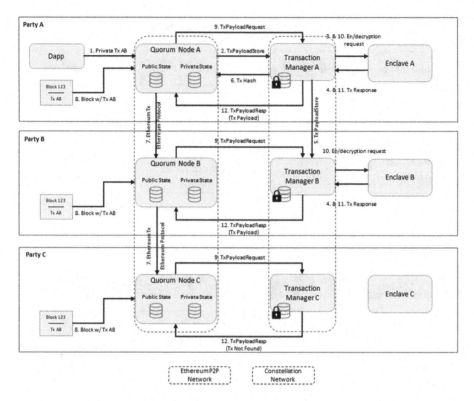

Figure 7-4. *Flow of Transactions on QuorumChain*

See: https://entethalliance.org/quorum-consortium-network-in-azure-marketplace.pdf

Ether.camp's Ethereum Studio Blockchain Environment

This option quickly sets up the development and deployment setup for Ethereum. It provides the template to write smart contracts and deploy them in a sandbox to test and emulate. It has an IDE to code the smart contracts and deploy them in an Ubuntu environment. The sandbox is a NodeJS server configuration that can emulate a multi-node network, thereby assisting with connecting nodes and governing based on the enforced smart contracts.

Ethereum on Azure by Microsoft/Parity Ethereum with Proof of Authority (PoA)

This toolkit utilizes the Ethereum virtual machine with proof of authority instead of PoW (proof of work) as shown in Figure 7-5. The governance is pre-defined.

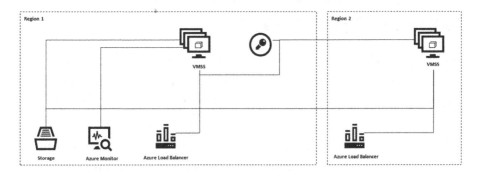

Figure 7-5. *Ethereum on Azure*

It contains the following Azure components (Figure 7-5):

- Virtual machines for running the PoA validators

- Azure Load Balancer for distributing RPC, peering, and governance DApp requests

- Azure Key Vault for securing the validator identities

- Azure Storage for hosting persistent network information and coordinating leasing

- Azure Monitor for aggregating logs and performance statistics

- VNet Gateway (optional) for allowing VPN connections across private VNets

Now that we have seen various architectures based on the variants that are outcomes of the 21-question matrix, let's drill down deeper to a component level of understanding from a developer's perspective and decide the suitability of the options.

Developer's Version of Technical Component Breakdown

Most major blockchain networks that are driven by public, private, or consortium networks are largely accepted due to the source code–level transparency of the platform. This establishes trust to implement and execute, thereby making it a trustworthy source for end users.

For example, Ethereum, Hyperledger, Corda, Quorum, NEM, Stellar, and so on all have made their frameworks open source and have further extended component codes on GitHub. This kind of setup allows businesses to integrate third-party frameworks in order to formulate blockchains with better confidence, as no loopholes are missed regarding the privacy and governance on-chain. The choice of development at this stage is most crucial.

The recipe here is for the solution architect to clearly focus on the components defined in the previous section. However, on a code level, severe scrutiny has to be maintained by the developer utilizing the proposed framework. For example, the 51% Miner's attack is one of the cases that was a loophole in Ethereum's earlier source code. However, its choice to move to proof of stake consensus ensures such attacks are avoided going forward.

For a developer, some of the most crucial elements are the toolkit provisions, programmatic inputs to develop the logical flow, and the choice of language. The sequence of decision to be made is recommended by focusing over the current infrastructure, business logic & then the choice of language that fits the first two. Why is the order of these elements crucial here?

- Infrastructural provisions – Because without the right set of infrastructural provisions, the most idealistic consensus may not work suitably for a business case that requires cloud components for large-scale outreach.

- Logical flows – Because the logical design and integration has to be correctly wired. For example, event registers and transaction watchers have to be logically wired during every transaction.

- Code language – This many times is driven by the community initiatives, such as those highlighting language affinity; for example, languages such as Go that enable Go developers to extend Go-Ethereum for several applications.

Since we are focused on the developer's version of technology tool selection for blockchains, let us consider the bottom-to-top approach (where bottom would be the back-end databases and the top would be the end users or front-end applications).

Layers of Tools

In a technology stack, every layer has specific functions, from the database end to the back end to the user interactivity in the front end. The layers of tools and the decisions based on functional components for a blockchain application are detailed next.

- Network peer-to-peer

- Core blockchain frameworks

- Privacy and scaling components

- Tooling elements

- Front-end elements

Network P2P Libraries

The following are some useful libraries:

a. Libp2p provides the package to set up peer networks. However, due to the developer alignment of language, it also has language implementation, such as the following:

   i. Go P2p

   ii. Kotlin-based P2P

   iii. Js-Lib p2p

   iv. Rust Lib p2p

b. Noise: P2P networking stack for developing decentralized applications and cryptographic protocols written in Go. This is used in Perlin Wavelet Network.

   i. Ref: `https://github.com/perlin-network/noise`

c. In Ethereum:

   i.   RLPx transport protocol: a TCP-based transport protocol used for communication among Ethereum nodes

   ii. Kademlia DHT (distributed hash table) provides peer selection during lookup, joining the network. The protocol contains four RPC—Ping, Store, Find Node, and Find Value.

d. In Quorum (which is available on the Azure Marketplace)

   i.   Network permissioning is a feature that controls which nodes can connect to a given node and also to which nodes the given node can dial out. Currently, it is managed at the individual node level by the `--permissioned` command-line flag when starting the node.

e. In the Ethereum Blockchain network on Azure:

   i.   The chain topology is deployed using the network virtual appliances (NVA).

   ii. NVAs maintain high availability behind load balancers and peer node servers, thus providing a fault-tolerant ecosystem

   iii. NVA IP addresses are used on-chain for a multi-node chain instead of the peer node's actual IP address, thus making it difficult to hack into a peer-to-peer environment.

f. Hyperledger Fabric:

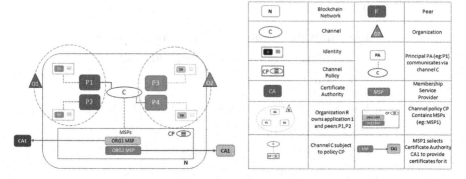

Figure 7-6. *Multi-Organization Peer-to-peer network in Hyperledger Fabric*

As we observe in Figure 7-6, the peer-to-peer network in Hyperledger Fabric runs on the chaincode defined by the network. This makes it flexible as well as focused on the purpose of the chain, along with the certificate authority issued by the participating organizations in a multi-node, multi-organization scenario.

Core Blockchain Frameworks

This section focuses on the components found inside the blockchain and not the elements around it. For example, it covers the consensus type, the network design for on-chain and off-chain activities, the logic of governance, and so on. The three main aspects are storage/ledger arrangement, execution, and consensus (Figure 7-7).

    a.   Microsoft Confidential Consortium Framework (CCF)

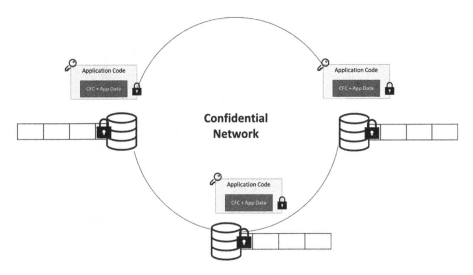

Figure 7-7. *Core Blockchain Frameworks*

i.   A framework to build secure, highly available, and performant applications that focus on multi-party computations and data

ii. It is not a blockchain itself, but enables the core components of a blockchain with the distributed ledgers, multi-party computing, and cryptography.

iii. The framework provides a TEE (trusted execution environment) wherein the code and data are locked with confidentiality and integrity in a secure place.

iv. It provides an Open Enclave SDK for developers to integrate in a TEE form for genuine decentralization and integrity of in-chain logic and data, as shown in Figure 7-8.

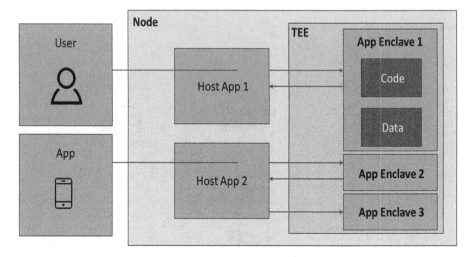

Figure 7-8. *Confidential Consortium Framework*

v. Usually while developing the consensus of any blockchain, the hard forks are kept limited and may not be changed ad hoc by the host unless accepted by all members. Therefore, the Open Enclave SDK provisions for that development credibility and stability. This makes the blockchain platform unbiased regarding the host/developer behind the platform once it is deployed on such a framework.

vi. Six prime elements of this framework are the following (Figure 7-8):

1. Hardware – SGX-enabled Azure Confidential Compute

2. Ledger – An append-only ledger provides encryption of the private data and serialization of the public data with a key-value pair store. The data is replicated on all nodes as the leader commits the transaction. The replication process currently uses Raft as the consensus algorithm.

3. Encryption – GCM (**Galois/Counter Mode**) by a key shared by all nodes for private data on-chain.

4. Governance – CCF allows its members to submit policies/proposals, which must be accepted by a quorum of members to be executed. The quorum is defined as a Lua script in the genesis transaction. Common governance operations include adding a new user, member, or version of the CCF code.

5. Key-Value Store structure of storing on-chain data, maps (tables), and transactions – It includes serialization and encryption. Also extends Key-Value Store APIs.

6. Recovery – CCF ensures recovery in case of extreme network failure where some transactions might not be copied in entirety. The restoration also occurs in true decentralized forms that must be accepted by all stakeholders involved in the loss of transaction data.

b. Frameworks for Ethereum: Truffle:

i.   Defined as a development environment, testing **framework**, and asset pipeline for Ethereum, aiming to make life as an Ethereum developer easier.

189

ii.   Microsoft's Visual Studio Code IDE provides Truffle Services along with Azure Cloud Services for an enhanced DevOps experience to develop and deploy Ethereum.

iii.   This framework has three main elements:

1. Truffle for smart contract development

2. Ganache for blockchain deployment for test environments

3. Drizzle – a redux store for fresh chain data for transaction execution and state of smart contract testing on the front end

iv.   Key takeaways for developers:

1. Ethereum developers can build logical smart contracts, deploy, and execute.

2. Mocha and Chai JS–based automated testing tools ensure proper coverage of smart contract codes.

3. Truffle supports JavaScript, SASS, ES6, and JSX, thereby allowing creativity of visuals as well as client-side contract actions.

4. Build management and pipelining

c.   Other frameworks such as Fabric, Sawtooth, Burrow, Iroha, or Indy provide crypto-agnostic options.

Privacy and Scaling Components

This section identifies the tools used for data privacy and details the components that can be used to scale towards better privacy measures on a blockchain platform.

a. Encryption

   i. Azure Media Services dynamically encrypt your content with AES 128-bit clear encryption keys.

   ii. Azure Storage automatically encrypts your data when persisting it to the cloud.

   iii. Azure Blockchain Service compiles these into secure encrypted components inside isolated virtual networks, making it difficult for a random hacker to identify the exact source of the data.

   iv. Data disks are encrypted by Azure Disk Encryption.

   v. Shared Access Signatures provide access on-chain for public assets.

   vi. For the blockchain quorum, Constellation provides a peer-to-peer message exchange system. It provides every node with key-generation capabilities and maintains a directory based on the privacy level of public or private networks.

b. Hashing

   i. Azure provides a serverless environment for such dynamic functions with the help of Azure logic apps and Flow.

   ii. Hashing may be implemented while onboarding digital assets on-chain with a hashed version of data and metadata.

    c.   Concurrency of Service Buses

        i.   Microsoft Azure Service Bus is a fully managed enterprise integration message broker.

        ii.   The service bus includes the queuing mechanisms, topic, and subscriptions.

Tooling Elements

    a.   Wallets

        i.   Ethereum blockchain interacts with several client-side wallets, such as Metamask, Ledger Nano X, Jaxx, etc., available for smartphones, other hardware, and desktop. These wallets are to transact on-chain.

        ii.   Hyperledger extends four types of wallets—File, In-Memory, HSM, and Database.

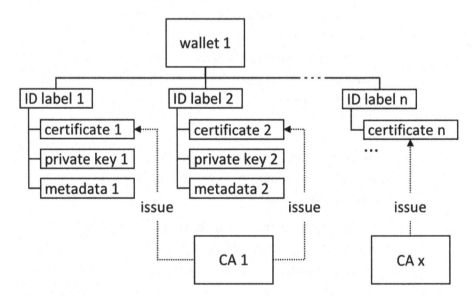

Figure 7-9. *Example: Layout of integration of wallets in a blockchain*

Front-end Elements

    a.   Applications

        i.   Truffle framework in the preceding list extends several front-end tools for smart contract deployments.

        ii.   Similarly, the Hyperledger Playground console provides a front end to visualize the transactions on-chain. The Hyperledger Composer Playground provides a user interface for the configuration, deployment and testing of a business network.

        iii.   Mobile development for Android and IOS on Xamarin and Azure help enhance wallet development on edge devices.

    b.   Block Explorers

        i.   With the amalgamation of all cloud components in the same ecosystem, a block explorer can be developed based on the transaction watchers and event grids on Azure.

        ii.   This would show the true status of the number of transactions, value of blocks, etc.

So far, we have covered the individual components of the blockchain stack for developer implementations and customizations. Let us further explore blockchain as a service tools for rapid deployments on Azure.

Blockchain as a Service

For this purpose, developers need to set up the Azure Dev Test Lab, which allows them to test these services and explore their suitability for the infrastructure defined by the solution architect.

Azure Dev Test Lab allows the following:

- Low-scale cloud setups for development purposes

- Pre-configured templates with quick environment setups

- Tools to integrate and scale

It includes the deployment of blockchain as a service options, such as the Blocknet for instance.

The Blocknet

This BaaS provides a lightweight option for having decentralized data be located across nodes on edge devices. It provides mobility, modularity, and interoperability. Have you ever wondered if a generic blockchain that creates copies on every node might take up too much space on each device? That is where Blocknet works like a decentralized exchange of data with a P2P atomic exchange protocol.

Further, to explore all the various options of technology that help to construct various use cases, challenges, and so forth, I recommend you check out other tooling services, such as OkCash, Ripple, Storj, BigChainDB, and others.

CHAPTER 8

Technical Architectures

This chapter will look at designing various constructs of blockchains and distributed ledgers in different use cases. After walking through an array of technological tools, the software architects, solution architects, and product design engineers have to generate architectures of blockchain elements either from scratch or on top of existing technology tools. This decision is usually based on the business requirements, technology choices, and developers' skills.

Architecture design of a software/application/platform or a network can be done at macro to micro levels based on the definition of the business use case. We shall divide the chapter based on the scale of the use case, starting with the macro level, moving to a domain-specific use case, and going to a micro-level design for automating smart contracts. Highlights of this chapter are as follows:

- **Designing**: In the first section, we will review the macroeconomics of the use case first, then define the business impact, and finally select the technology stack for assembling a blockchain for trade finance.

- **Defining**: In the second section, the wide frame from the last section will be reduced to a narrower use case, one specific to a particular function and not the entire economy and ecosystem. The stakeholders are finite, and the functional dependency is highly reduced.

© Shilpa Karkeraa 2020
S. Karkeraa, *Unlocking Blockchain on Azure*,
https://doi.org/10.1007/978-1-4842-5043-3_8

- **Implementing**: In the third section, we will examine the technology stacks for smart contracts, including the legal frameworks for various geographical locations that recognize them and the requirements to adhere to the conditions of the smart contracts.

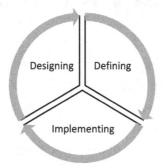

Figure 8-1. *Core fundamental process of designing architectures for a blockchain platform*

The core fundamental process of developing architectures for a successful blockchain platform is an iterative process, as shown in Figure 8-1. It requires continuous review of the design based on the feedback of implementations.

With the guidelines of Chapter 7, one can establish the structure of the use case at hand using the CAUSE Matrix, 21 Question Set, and the GHOSSTTT Protocol. The key components of consideration for any software platform for which we will plan and design architectures in this chapter with respect to blockchains are as follows:

- Measure of scales with respect to user base, locations, entities, objects, etc.

- Functional density and coverage

- Functionality and scalability (depth-wise and breadthwise)

- Computation complexity plus hardware dependencies

- Core decisions toward implementations

- Tools to support scale and maintenance

- Frameworks

- On-chain and off-chain combinations of architecture design

Let's call these the **8D factors of architecture**.

Designing a Blockchain Solution Architecture for Trade Finance

The first step is to identify all key stakeholders that may interact with the trade finance blockchain platform. Enlist the stakeholders and decide the role of the user, whether they will be a full node or a contributor to the node or an off-chain member. In this use case, where we look at the world-trade application at a macro level, we must consider the following players:

- Exporter/seller

- Importer/buyer

- Issuing bank

- Nominated bank

- Advising bank

- Chain of banks/branches involved in the verification process

- Intermediaries such as shipper, customs, procurement companies

197

In a global trade scenario (as shown in Figure 8-2), there will be a lot more trade players—governmental, regulatory, customs, different shipments, and so on. However, to design the global trade application on a blockchain, we shall simplify the trade process for learning purposes. Once that is clear, one can add many types of players and define their roles on the chain. The onboarding of such players will be similar to the fundamentals explained in this section.

The Global Trade Chain

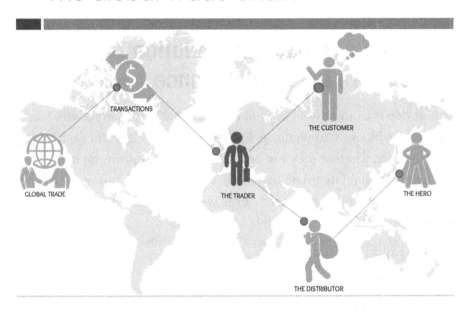

Figure 8-2. *Global trade players*

This may vary case to case. Here, we look at it in the crudest form that a beginner would view and understand. From there on, it is an iterative process to refine the architecture design based on the maturity of the platform, the stakeholders, and the positioning of the core functions of the chain.

In trade finance, let's identify a challenge that really may need a blockchain. We must consider the credibility of the trade players. Many large-value trades default, either in payments or in delivery of the trade items. Trade finance brings letters of credit and bank guarantees by financial institutions to be catalysts for credible trade.

First Challenge

A letter of credit (LoC), also known as a documentary credit or bankers commercial credit, or letter of undertaking (LoU), is a payment mechanism used in international trade to provide an economic guarantee from a creditworthy bank to an exporter of goods (see Figure 8-3).

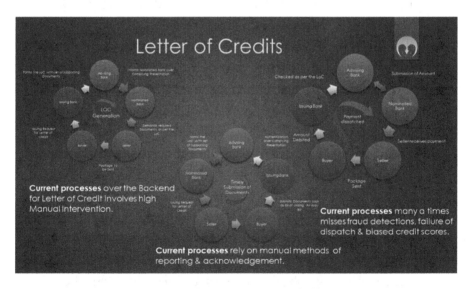

Figure 8-3. *Usual Process of Letter of Credit generation across institutions*

Traditionally, financial institutions were the centralized source of trust, therefore the concept of LoCs. However, in recent times, there have been cases of default despite such documents due to hackers being able to hack into bank systems, or manual intervention being undertaken by staff/contractual third-party collaborations, and so forth.

This centralized trust can surely be scaled up with the more secure practices of blockchains. When a bank commissions and outsources the development of its digital systems to a company, if on a blockchain, the trust and transparency are maintained regarding the inclusion of said company. Many may disagree that such transparency allows for better practices. Therefore, during the design of a blockchain for the trade finance chain, one may choose the type of blockchain and its activities.

However, one element of security is ensured, for a hacker to hack into a centralized server is lot less computationally intensive than to hack into a whole decentralized blockchain network. So with blockchains, we do not directly call for the removal of intermediaries. Many times blockchains facilitate more transparent and credible practices.

Now that the design is established, we shall dissect the use case for blockchains in trade finance for letters of credit. Starting with who initiates the onboarding of other players among the listed set of trade players? Why would anyone agree to join a transparent blockchain ledger? How many businesses still avoid having an online presence?

Therefore, the first challenge of design is **onboarding mechanisms**.

Since a bank or a financial institute is deemed to be a credible source by all majority trade players, it may be logistically easier to initiate onboarding with banks. However, this is not a hard and fast rule. One may initiate onboarding industry-wise; for example, one can start with the onboarding of farmers and consumers and plug other players in gradually. so based on the players involved in a transaction for a business, the decentralized platform may choose the onboarding mechanism.

Points of consideration for onboarding mechanisms:

- Consensus required for onboarding?

- Onboarding user and onboarding node the same?

- Pre-requisites required for onboarding of member?

- Who is enabled to onboard after the initial onboarding?

All the answers to the preceding questions entirely depend on the business, challenge, and purpose of the chain. In our siloed case of consideration, we allow the financial institute to onboard an initial set of members. Members can further onboard other trade players that satisfy the on-chain consensus conditions. Every user is a node, making it truly decentralized end to end.

Second Challenge

Once the onboarding mechanism is chosen, but before onboarding the members, the solution architect needs to ensure all activities/transactions follow the common rule of consensus defined before any onboarding. For example, when a set of smart contract rules are validated, only then can the defined activity take place, or can be the proof of stake where the majority of stakeholders decide the activity to execute or to decline. In a consortium of private and public blockchains, there can be more than one form of consensus in the blockchain, each pertaining to the private or public blockchain.

Therefore, the second challenge of design is **choice of consensus mechanisms**.

One of the original reasons for forming the blockchain was credibility; therefore, the consensus mechanism needs to ensure that the credibility of the trade players is transparently tracked and maintained on-chain. Points of consideration may be identified throughout the book where consensus mechanisms are defined, or one can develop one's own mechanism.

For the current use case, we chose a combination of proof of work and proof of stake, along with the conditions of the smart contract that create the value of credibility that will govern the overall trade trust.

Once consensus is defined in the blockchain, onboarding to private/ public blockchain consortiums can begin. The public blockchain may host all peer nodes that trade or are involved in trade. The private blockchain may be formed ad-hoc or synced whenever trade is initiated, and only those trade players may be included.

Third Challenge

During onboarding, the Know-Your-Customer (KYC) may be required as per the design, along with the peer node validation. This is similar to a referral from friends/family or a validation from a bank.

Post-onboarding of trade players, one has to assign the role they will undertake on chain.

The third challenge of design is **assignment of roles to nodes**.

Roles to assign in a blockchain may be as follows as we observe in Figure 8-4:

- Client Nodes – End users that onboard when they require a service on the chain. In our current use case, it is the importer and exporter (i.e., buyer and seller).

- Peer Nodes – The banks that the end users deal with need to be on-chain permanently. The issuing and nominated bank branches may be identified as peer nodes. Certain peer nodes can be endorser nodes. For example, the issuing bank endorses the exporter's credibility, initiates a transaction, and maintains the state of his credibility.

- Orderer Nodes – These nodes are the conveyers of transactions, validating unbiasedly to ensure the delivery of the transaction activity in a fault-tolerant way. Therefore, by design, the architect needs to ensure the ratio proportion of peer nodes and orderer nodes is appropriate to avoid bias imbalance.

Further, CA nodes could be authorizers of these roles and assign powers associated with these roles. This authority by CA forms consensus by proof of stake to maintain the permissioned ledger aspect.

Also, the KYC of client nodes could be a separate blockchain with proof of identity consensus, if required. This again depends on the focus of the platform provider. Otherwise, the CA nodes can ensure the onboarding validations.

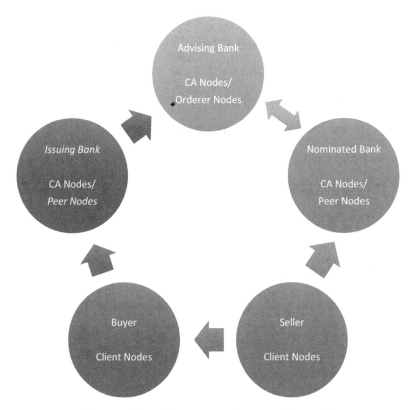

Figure 8-4. *Assigning the roles to members on-boarding*

Fourth Challenge

After the assignment of roles, the platform requires the definition of the data structures and transaction activities.

The fourth design challenge is to define **on-chain data structures and transaction activities**.

Here, the definition is scoped based on the focus of the letters of credit and the regulations around them.

Data points identified in this scenario are as follows:

- Document inputs, such as KYC, bill of lading, etc.

- Document verification status

- Majority voting status

- Conditions of the smart contracts

Transaction activity points are defined as follows:

- Validation of documents

- Transfer of documents

- Approval of smart contract conditions

- Payment dispatch on majority status

For detailed planning, one can phase out all stages as follows:

FEATURES	Description
Node generation, integration, and chain setup	• Creation of nodes (KYC/ AML) • Access control • Link generation • Sequence locking • Document machine translation to smart contracts • Self-authentication

(continued)

FEATURES	Description
Smart contracts for letters of credit (LoC) and bank guarantees (BG)	• LoC smart contract request form • BG smart contract request form • Auto-verification of smart contract across nodes • Transfer of documents through chain • Validation and alerts • Smart triggers as per contract
Transactions and other actionables	• Real-time money dispatch on honoring LoC smart contract • Loss settlement on withholding bank guarantee • Alert on various document updates • Warning alerts on low credits and fraud detections
Monitoring panel	• Node view as per access control • Authorization control • Validation controls • Reports and alerts

Fifth Challenge

To get further clarity and the predictability of a complete design, one must ensure the blockchain covers all cases. So, the next design challenge is ensuring full functional coverage.

The fifth design challenge is to implement a **full-coverage blockchain** code.

To ensure full coverage of the blockchain code, one needs to define all possible user stories between every type of user. Let us identify the buyer side (Figure 8-5) and seller side of functionalities (Figure 8-6).

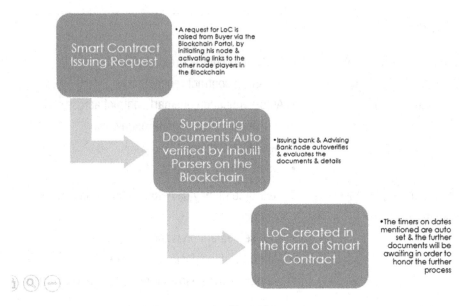

Figure 8-5. *User stories on the buyer side*

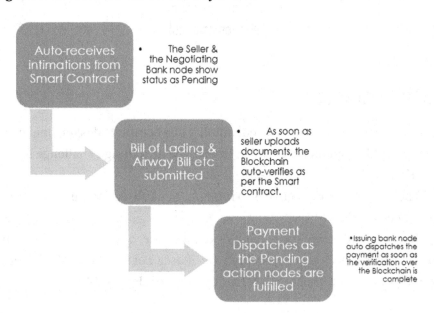

Figure 8-6. *User stories on the seller side*

The banking nodes are CA nodes, and there are validator nodes with different levels of authority. As shown in Figure 8-7.

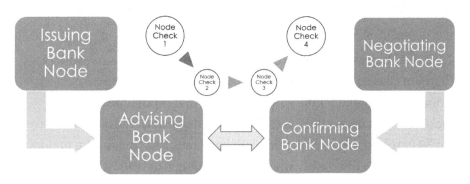

Figure 8-7. *Validation and transaction activity between banking nodes*

Remember: As an architect or a developer or a blockchain platform provider, one has the responsibility to design and develop a full proof so as to avoid any loopholes, bypasses, and centralization opportunities. These issues are entertained in a centralized platform as one can keep updating without any consensus of the subscribers. However, corrections and updates on a blockchain get computationally complicated due to the consensus required to accept the change and update the local nodes. Thus arose the concept of forking.

Forking is defined in various ways based on the situation, as follows:

- what happens when a blockchain diverges into two potential paths forward

- a change in protocol

- a situation that occurs when two or more blocks have the same block height

- a situation where contradictory loopholes are found or race condition–like situations occur

For example, when the number of users in the trustless network of Ethereum Classic (proof of work) increased, vulnerability increased, leading to a 51 percent attack. It is an attack that is possible on a blockchain that uses a PoW algorithm for consensus if the attackers have over 50 percent control of the network hash rate. That means the majority of the network is filled with attackers that validate and allow fraudulent transactions, causing the attack. Such loopholes are to be pre-envisioned to avoid security breaches.

This makes the fifth challenge the most crucial, that is ensuring the core attributes of a blockchain are foolproof. How does one ensure that? Fill in the following table with the pain point, issues around the pain point, node responsibilities in those situations, and the solution action as a whole for the transaction, as shown in Figure 8-8.

PROBLEM	ISSUES	SOLUTION PROCESSES					SOLUTION ACTION
		Node 1 BUYER	Node 2 ISSUING BANK	Node 3 ADVISING BANK	Node 4 NOMINATED BANK	Node 5 SELLER	
LoC Generation	• Slow Process • Manual Intervention • Longer process of Intimation	Node Initiator	Node Linked	Node Linked	Node Intimated	Node Requested	• Transparent records on the ledger by nodes involved in the LoC. • Auto-intimation of players involved to form Smart Contracts • Real Time Action • Low/ Minimum manual intervention
Document Verification	• High dependency on matching records correctly • Bottlenecked by untimely scheduling or document delivery by parties involved	Document Inputs Uploaded	Auto verify & Translated	Auto verified **LoC** Issued Smart Contract Generated	Node Acknowledged	Node accepted	• Intuitive Verification by NLP & Smart Parsers • Ontology Models that interpret different formats
Biased Credits & Different Jurisdictions	• On fulfillment of documents by Seller, sometimes, the LoC is dishonored due to Biased Credits & mismatch of regulations as per jurisdictions • Causing larger issues of Settlements	Insufficient Funds – Unable to make payment	Credit Score Calculation as per Guidelines by Smart Parsers	Rejects LoC Request	Intimates Bank real time about the status	Seller cancels dispatch	• Credit Authenticator automates credit score calculation • Includes the jurisdictional interest while forming the Smart Contract
Tracking Fraud Patterns	• Documents submitted to Regulatory Bodies are not real time & well archived • No Intuitive patterns can be queried from current records directly	Document Inputs Uploaded	Auto verify & Translated	LoC Created	Alerts the time of Upload & required documents	Receives updates	• First round of Consensus Algorithm approves all activities and generates LoC as per regulations • Second Round is dispatched as soon as LoC is Honored. • These patterns can be universally tracked with intuitive checkers for known loop holes for money laundering • With the real time updated ledger the records are always up-to date. Thus causing high transparency to Regulatory Bodies to detect fraud easily.
		Auto Dispatch of Payment	Approves payment dispatch	LoC Approved & Honored	Verifies uploaded documents as per contract	Uploads all required documents - Bill of Lading, Custom Bills	

Figure 8-8. Solution: user stories for all cases

209

EXERCISE

Fill in the following table for a decentralized inventory system such that it avoids high inventory costs and minimizes stock-out loss.

PROBLEM	ISSUES	PROCESS ALLOCATION			SOLUTION ACTION
		Node Type 1	Node Type 2	Node N	

As we can see in Figure 8-9, the buyer and seller are subscribers of an intermediary and avail themselves of the services of the financial institution. Being subscribers of the service, the equation of authority, transparency, and decision-making is not really in their control. Whereas, when all users come onto a decentralized platform, it enables the user to advocate and involve himself in the decision-making.

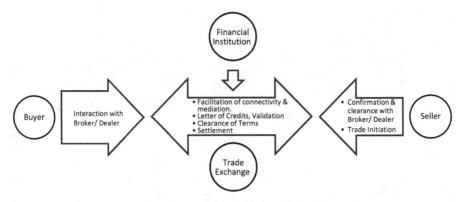

Figure 8-9. *Centralized conventional flow of trade finance*

For example, as we see in Figure 8-10, the nodes such as validator, peer, and orderer are the transacting stakeholders, which jointly validate a transaction based on the consensus binded it.

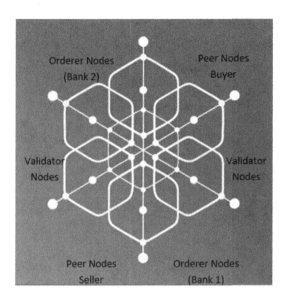

Figure 8-10. *Decentralized flow of trade finance*

Note that this arrangement is a consortium of various blockchains. Some between organizations, some within organizations. For example, the public chain across all stakeholders will be inter-organization, where multiple parties are involved in the trade. Many times, a node representative will be an organization representative that requires internal consensus to perform an action on the public chain. So, whenever the private chain in an internal organization is forming consensus, that is when the node representative validates the transaction on the public chain, thereby maintaining full end-to-end transparency and connectivity.

Sixth Challenge

The final design challenge is to arrange the elements in the architecture based on decisions identified in Chapter 7 and in the preceding pain points.

The sixth design challenge is to draw out the **consolidated architecture stack**.

In the trade finance use case, we have stacked the key components of the services required.

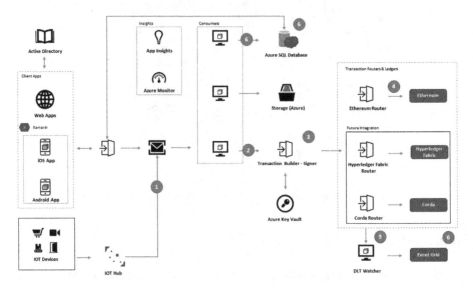

Figure 8-11. *A consolidated architecture stack with all components*

The consolidated stack comprises the end-to-end touchpoints, ranging from edge devices such as IoT integrations to the event grid that triggers events based on the smart contract or consensus (Figure 8-11).

Figure 8-12 shows a collaborative workflow aiming for true decentralization.

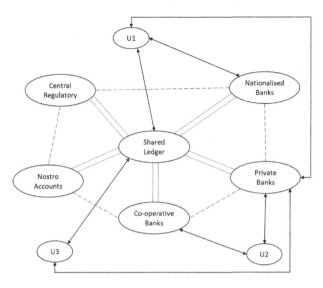

Figure 8-12. *Enterprise positioning of financial institutions involved in global trade finance*

There are three levels of design:

- system architecture

- enterprise architecture

- application architecture

Refer to Figures 8-13 and 8-14 for sample architecture flows typically in a financial services environment.

System architecture lets you place the physical and virtual components of the blockchain across the network with respect to hardware (such as virtual machines on cloud, computers, servers, mobile phones, smart devices) as well as its integration with the software service layers hosted.

Enterprise architecture is a model that allows enterprise structure and functionalities to be embedded in the process of the application. Here, the design is focused on what the components do, and not how they work. This enables different sections of enterprise teams to interact and integrate. TOGAF and Zachman frameworks exist across enterprises, and blockchain designs can take references to the existing models and improvise.

213

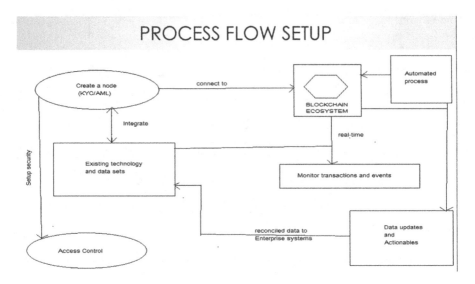

Figure 8-13. *Process flow for setup of blockchain in financial institutions*

Application architecture walks through the functional components specific to the application. The focus area must cover the chain service mechanism for transaction activity, contract definitions and translations, triggers and alerts, stake division, permissions, and so forth.

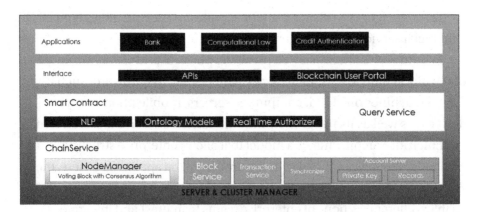

Figure 8-14. *Application set up in a financial services environment*

Now that we have learned the different types of architecture and their application-based designs, let us look into the 8D Factors of Technical Architecture defined at the start of this chapter.

Measure of Scale with Respect to User Base, Locations, Entities, and Objects

User Base and Locations

In trade finance, the user base includes a global canvas of people ranging from traders, buyers, exporters, and international agencies, to customs, regulatory bodies, countries, financial institutions, vetting bodies, and so on. At the same time, it includes local micro-chains of producers, transport companies, cooperative banks, agro distributors, packaging companies, financial micro lenders, local governmental schemes and bodies, and so forth that work around the local environment. As a blockchain platform, one may cover local or global areas—it depends on the problem that the platform wishes to solve.

For example, if financial inclusion is the focus of the chain, it must start locally and spread to remote areas to which access is limited. When global financial inclusion is the focus, the blockchain platform must connect all remote areas globally and include trade aggregators to accelerate outreach. One may incentivize these peer nodes to onboard remote trade players. The question that may arise is, why include all such players while considering trade finance? When the end-to-end players are completely connected by a decentralized platform, information is a lot more credible than when you have biased sources of information offline or on centralized online platforms. With such credible information on this immutable ledger, better-informed decisions and predictive factors can be calculated. The proof of credit can be tangibly measured; you'll have not just the validation of one node or a group of nodes but also the tamper-proof history on the blockchain ledger.

An architect developing the design for such a platform needs to factor in the scale of the user base based on the short-term and long-term goals of the business service. Similarly, the locations of global, local, and remote entities have to be decided in order to shape the technology stack around them. Further, with the consideration of location, one has to factor in the socioeconomic status of the user's locale. For example, places without proper internet access might need to be part of fault-tolerant networks so that if validation does not get approved by every user due to a lack of internet, operations could still continue. The architect has to maintain the right ratio of validator nodes, peer nodes, and orderer nodes for a functional network with the right forms of consensus mechanisms. Also, the architect must choose the device form based on location; for example, field specialists such as farmers and fishermen might not have computer access, and therefore those nodes might have to be on a virtual cloud server node or mobile device node or a camera node that could be an IoT device connected to the blockchain.

Entities and Objects

With platform of several entities involved in a trade finance blockchain, the regulations, IT policies, and access control may differ from entity to entity. If it is a collaborative network, to have appropriate consensus, all factors of the various entity policies have to be covered. For example, a cooperative bank or a financial institution needs to maintain its Azure Active Directory in a particular way; the format has to remain as is. Azure provides a mapping between the enterprise's Active Directory to the blockchain's user directory. A blockchain integration may run over multiple Azure accounts with their independent AD policies. This mapping to the blockchain's directory is crucial to the design. At the same time, a node from one entity must not be able to access other entities' ADs in any way.

Objects may be assets, contracts, data structures, off-chain reports, and so forth. However, there have been several fintech hacks in the cryptocurrency markets resulting from improper security of off-chain wallets. So, in a trade finance network, if the validation circuit is on-chain, and the downloadable report can be modified off-line without a hash address trace, then the entire point of having such a validation on-chain is invalid. So, the architect must question whether a blockchain is truly required while constructing every object, both on-chain and off-chain. Azure securely maintains monitoring systems, event triggers, and off-chain stores to trace objects.

The measure of scale could be as small as a three-entity local blockchain network for trade finance or as large as a million-entity global blockchain network for global trade finance. However, maintaining the decentralization and consensus along with the core fundamentals of the blockchain is extremely crucial at every stage. At the same time, once established and processes are set up on-chain, one can expand the transaction activity from one object to several objects (assets) and scale functionalities.

Functional Density and Coverage

Functional density could be based on adding more players to the chain for a particular function or increasing functional responsibility for a few players in the chain. At the same time, certain functions may be irrelevant to the core challenge of credibility and may be taken offline.

To be exact, letters of credit process validation may go through several internal processes within an entity. So, does one add all players in the same chain or create a separate private chain for this internal process? Similarly, when user inclusion is decided for the trade finance blockchain service, is the selection of users wider or highly niche? This defines the type of users in the coverage.

Functionality and Scalability (Depth-wise and Breadthwise)

Once the definitions of the first two factors are clear, one has to map the technical aspects based on the defined functionality and scalability. For example, when there are thousands of features on a blockchain, with limited scalability, the time-lags are well adjusted. However, would the same source code for the blockchain suffice for a billion-user base? The vision of functional depth and breadth with respect to user-base scalability has to be clear so as to avoid several hard forks. When Azure components form parts of the blockchain, such as event grids, compute servers, and AD-based authentications, the scalability issues are modularized and can be easily taken care of in silos.

Computation Complexity Plus Hardware Dependencies

The form of consensus method chosen has a crucial impact on the hardware computation and memory. Every node has to be active for a blockchain, which causes an expectation of high up-time from all nodes, leading to an eventual bottleneck. The selection of a consensus algorithm based on the scale definitions helps to identify the hardware dependencies.

Alternatively, businesses may start with planning for hardware limitations before doing the platform design, which is the step where consensus algorithms have to be selected. Based on this step and the affordability of the majority user base.

Core Decisions for Implementations

When certain limitations are discovered—for example, the proof of work reduced a stakeholder's influence on decisions—such decisions have to be a hard rule on-chain. When a chain is governed by proof of stake, one has to decide to ensure all transaction activity follows that very standard set of procedures.

Tools to Support Scale and Maintenance

Azure components speed deployments and node inclusion in most cases. The maintenance of services on-chain is taken care of by the cloud service provider. At the same time, one must carefully measure the computation versus tool costs to enable blockchain services.

Frameworks

Blockchain frameworks such as Ethereum, Hyperledger, Corda, and Ripple can be easily integrable with the Azure components, making sure deployment is faster and scalable. Based on the choice of scale, locale, and form of consensus, one can choose the desired framework.

On-chain and Off-chain Combinations of Architecture Design

Since the trade finance blockchain network traverses through several organizations and entities, certain elements will always be off-chain. For example, the core AD values of authentication will be centrally controlled only by the organization owning it. Democratizing those elements on-chain is irrelevant in this blockchain. Similarly, SAP or other existing ERP data where the intermediate state of data is irrelevant do not have to be hosted over blockchains. Therefore, identifying elements, data structures, and assets both on-chain and off-chain is one of the most crucial aspects of design.

Defining a Content Distribution Blockchain Architecture for Content Tracking, Licensing, and Royalties

Getty Images and Shutterstock deliver image content with their licenses and use rights. Similarly, Spotify ensures connectivity to independent artists' content that is catered to end users. These centralized platforms provision accessibility. However, the problem of piracy remains a large concern. Many movie scripts and screenplays have been plagiarized, with no order or control. Such data leaks were often not traceable, as the storage of machine addresses was not a common practice. Now, in this era, when global places are getting closer, a copied film script from one country is easily identifiable in a faraway country. However, such traceability is partly done online and partly offline due to the manual intervention involved.

Similar to the case of fake news, fraudulent data contributors make it hard to identify fake patterns due to mismanagement of the data's traceability. This does not mean centralized platforms do not have traceability, but it was never a prime concern. The traceability can be maintained in centralized platforms. However, it is highly tamperable. Enter blockchains.

This makes it an interesting use case, where genuine data sharing is of true value and there is equal contribution throughput and returns for such data. So, content providers are directly incentivized based on the data's value. This is even seen in many of today's content platforms, such as YouTube, Instagram, and so forth. However, as the platform scales, it becomes very difficult to identify the genuineness of the platform content. The effort to identify fake content on such platforms costs platform providers time & resources as well as a case of mis-identity for genuine content creators.

Blockchains maintain traceability from source to destination with every digital copy. Think of it as a digital signature of the artist/content creator that moves with the asset. When a document of data is shared with someone over Google Drive, one could create a copy, modify, tamper with it, and share it further. The original ownership and data about royalties are lost with such forms of sharing. Also, such centralized services expose the content over the network, as there is no upfront assurance of end-to-end encryption in such cases. So, we need blockchains.

With end-to-end encryption and the transfer of assets with the digital signatures of the content creators, traceability can always be maintained with blockchains. Apart from traceability, it is the access to incentives that could happen in real time or more transparently and fairly on blockchains that makes them appealing. For example, in a centralized content-management platform like Twitch, where gamers who stream their game videos get paid between one cent and one dollar an hour based on popularity and viability for advertisements, the incentives are paid when certain conditions as per the rules of the platform are fulfilled and the disbursements are made as per company policy at the sole discretion of the company. In such situations, the content-hosting company has full ownership of the authority and incentives and may regulate value and policy as they wish without taking consensus or agreement from the content creators. Now, imagine if there were a blockchain-based content-sharing platform that distributed hosting and content-creation responsibilities to client nodes, orderer nodes for host sharing and load balancing, and validation nodes to validate the content distributions. On such a platform, sharing, distribution, and incentive-sharing would be based on true blockchain consensus. Only then would the action of viewing, redistribution, and payments be triggered. Also, the value of the incentives could be more transparent with respect to profit-sharing and the agreed upon value, as per consensus.

A simpler example of decentralized profit distribution among content creators and nodes that enable distribution is based on the proof of work; i.e., energy spent on creating the content, distributing the content, and the demand over the content (Figure 8-15). Once this value is tangible in the form of paid subscriptions and advertisement eyeballs, the company may profit share fairly based directly on the varying amounts of profit. This ensures faster outreach, faster feedback, and faster disbursals.

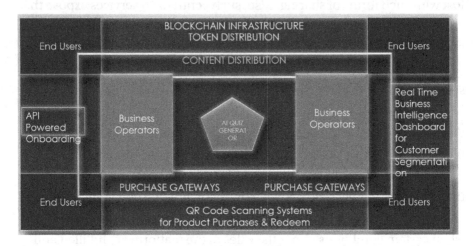

Figure 8-15. *Content-distribution platform architecture powered with AI on blockchains*

In the preceding arrangement, end-to-end users are connected in different blockchains of private and public ledgers based on the content-distribution rights agreed to on-chain. For example, if certain content is exclusive to certain business operators, it remains encrypted (appears garbled to others), and the decryption key is only on the receivers' address. However, if a business operator wishes to resell or license the content further, the consensus of trade between this business entity and the content provider may be agreed upon via a smart contract and can be taken forward for reselling and profit-sharing accordingly. So, when A creates content, B resells that content to C, and D views and interacts with A's content, the traceability of source to destination records is maintained on the blockchain ledger (Figure 8-16).

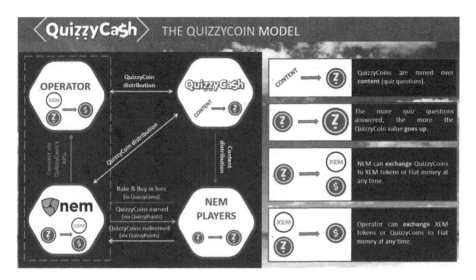

Figure 8-16. *Quizzycash: a content-distribution platform that measures proof of engagement on blockchains*

So, a blockchain company called QuizzyCash runs on the consensus of proof of customer engagement. Every content value is incentivized based on its measure of customer/user engagement. In simpler terms, if there is an important English Premier League match coming up and the latest quiz has relevant content, the traction of customer engagement may be high, yielding high advertisement values and thereby incentivizing the creator proportionally. This was developed based on NEM's framework of proof of importance. The token mechanics are generated based on the desired measure and distribution.

Technical architectures of existing frameworks can always be modified to fit the application, enterprise, and system architectures.

The following table analyzes the 8D Factors of Architecture for the content-distribution use case.

Factor	Impact
1. Measure of scale with respect to user base, locations, entities, objects, etc.	User base could largely vary based on geolocations and the market size. For example, Netflix has a huge consumer base in India; therefore, the value return for content targeted toward a location could become more transparent to the content creator directly. Similarly, when content agencies are involved in deals with content distributors, many times payments are stuck in spite of profitable deliveries. Here, blockchains enable entities to be involved in fair trade based on auto-executing smart contracts. Similar types of content can be stored on the blockchain ledgers, such as movies, artworks, books, etc.
2. Functional density and coverage	Functional density could be based on the content generators' impact which measures beyond mere advertisement fees and subscription rates. It may extend to neuroscience impact in a region or a country as well as the coverage of impact from various demographics.
3. Functionality + scalability (depth-wise and breadthwise)	A blockchain architect for such a platform has to decide the direction of breadth of features or its depth based on the user base during its initial phase through the growth phase. Similarly, scalability is to be decided.
4. Computation complexity plus hardware dependencies	Once functionality and scalability are locked, the computational complexity of passing content is to be calculated. Is it entirely the content itself on the blockchain, or just a pointer reference of the content? For example, having movies or art pieces on a blockchain would makes it storage-wise intensive, as several copies make it bulky. Complexity calculations enable one to forecast the node server's running costs, and so the incentive plans of distribution must fairly account for it.

(continued)

Factor	Impact
5. Core decisions toward implementations	Core decisions are similar to rules that the platform as a whole must abide by. For example, the blockchain ledger does not allow free ticket content to be added on the platform.
6. Tools to support scale and maintenance	Once identified that the gradual scale and functional coverage may change, one has to plan the hard and soft forks of updates or include them in the consensus agreements during onboarding.
7. Frameworks	The current example was built on top of NEM.
8. On-chain and off-chain combinations of architecture design	On-chain – Content uploads, redistributions, third-party integrations Off-chain – Storage of large-scale content repository

Implementing Architectures for Legal Smart Contracts

This section does not educate on the legal aspect for any country in particular for smart contracts; it mainly targets the logical flows and the enablers.

Smart contracts mainly come from the Ethereum framework of proof of work (Figure 8-17).

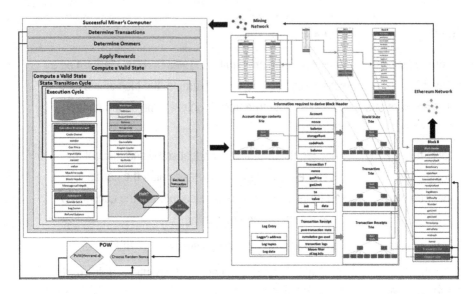

Figure 8-17. *Detailed flow of PoW in Ethereum*

Further understanding the Ethereum technical architecture and how to make it adaptive to the system, enterprise, and application architectures is highly crucial. The puzzle-solving in Ethereum generally enables the proof of work. Similarly, the legal framework of trade transactions or dealerships requires a well-defined smart contract for all cases, as well as consensus.

Here, the application of auto-enforceable and -executable smart contracts may vary from land ownerships, leases, and real estate dealerships, to insurance claims and financial proceedings. Smart contracts may execute different slabs of insurance premiums based on the style of driving a person may have, rather than based on standard values.

So, the design of an architecture can include the Ethereum/ Hyperledger framework along with the Truffle integrations for wallets and the Solidity execution for smart contracts.

EXERCISE

Similar to the learnings for the first two sections, compute the 8D Factors of Architecture for automobile service contract management.

CHAPTER 9

Use Cases

Over the course of this book, we have drilled into various aspects of
blockchains as well as use cases to help us focus on those aspects. In
this chapter, we will take a step up and view the array of possibilities of
use cases that were executed in various industries for various purposes.
As we walk through this journey of use cases and the experience of
building and executing some, the reader is required to refer back over the
initial chapters to correlate the elements of blockchain and to map the
appropriate tools, architectures, consensus, and so on. If a particular use
case uses a particular stack, one can always challenge with better protocols
and architectures to yield better throughputs and performances.

And as we upskill ourselves and improve our capabilities and our
understanding to create, implement, and manage blockchain-based
applications, we need to look around and understand the current use
cases under implementation. Insight into such active use cases will give us
a detailed understanding of the context in which blockchains can be used.
Along with this, we will also be looking into some of the active use cases
that have been developed for different industries and how Microsoft Azure
Blockchain has been transforming the world from transport to trade.

While the preceding description of the chapter may seem daunting
and like a lot of work, and make you feel like grabbing a cup of coffee
to replenish your mind and energy, it would be fun for you to know
that now even coffee and blockchains are related. This comes from
Microsoft Azure's collaboration with Starbucks, one of the world's leading

© Shilpa Karkeraa 2020
S. Karkeraa, *Unlocking Blockchain on Azure*,
https://doi.org/10.1007/978-1-4842-5043-3_9

coffeehouses, and how their efforts have brought in more transparency and experientiality to the entire generation of third-wave coffee drinkers.

To understand this example better and to look at more such fascinating examples, let's explore how blockchains have made the world a better place through the following examples:

- Decentralized customer engagement

- Decentralized trade finance

- Document signing and records management

- Distributed entity such as content

Decentralized Customer Engagement

Attracting and engaging customers and giving them the best customer experience is one of the key focus areas of any business, be it a small corner shop or a megastore like Walmart. While this equation has been relevant since the time the traders took to the Silk Route to sell goods from China to the Middle East, the mechanisms and appeal of the customer experience keep changing with economics, market conditions, and customer maturity. We will explore two use cases in depth to understand how blockchains helped these companies stand out when it came to customer experience.

Bill'U: Your Personal ERP

Bill'U is a Singapore-based enterprise blockchain platform focusing on the experience of retail customers to enhance their shopping experience by digitizing shopping receipts and warranty cards.

Bill'U, a.k.a. TechMyBill.com, provides a decentralized peer-to-peer bill-sharing platform. It is an expense ledger of billing documents, such as bills, coupons, vouchers, warranties, user manuals, and so forth—a one-stop-shop solution to managing all billing documents securely. It allows users to create, scan, share, and store documents on the ledger. This cutting-edge platform has two of development tracks: research specific and application specific.

Blockchain research makes the platform a highly secure environment for retailers, customers, and all stakeholders to securely manage all their billing documents. Unlike the conventional options of mail or an online service that brokers user data, Bill'U brings end-to-end encryption and provides complete ownership of user data for all stakeholders involved. This part of the platform does not directly interact with the users in terms of features. However, data being the core asset, the presence of such a mesh of private and public blockchains is extremely crucial in terms of data security and data sensitivity. We shall elaborate the constructs of this in the use case below.

The application side of Bill'U embeds artificial intelligence to make the numbers more human readable and usable. Imagine reminders of your expiring coupons that always go unused or renewal of warranties so as to be covered for any damages. All bill documents on the ledger can be searched intelligently with the "ASK Bill'U" feature. The user can ask questions about grocery costs, monthly travel expenses, or any queries about the uploaded expenses.

The blockchain ledger and the AI-enabled application make Bill'U the next-generation platform for all billing documents.

Every node (over an edge device—mobile, desktop, or a cloud account) uploads bills/scans digital QR Bills that are locally preserved as the first reference. The AI is locally embedded inside each node. Every such node participates in the blockchain ecosystem. The data that is authorized to be shared anonymously flows onto the public blockchain, whereas when a consumer purchases an item from a retailer, the specific information that is confidential is encrypted and shared over the private chain exclusive to the rightful stakeholder.

Figure 9-1 shows how it works.

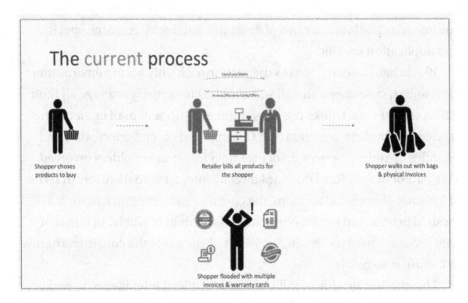

Figure 9-1. *The current offline process of billing for a retail customer*

You must have experienced a similar process while shopping, and along with shopping bags and happy memories of the day, you would have ended up with a lot of unwanted, difficult-to-manage receipts. The major disadvantages of this conventional setup are shown in Figure 9-2.

Challenges in the status quo

	No digital invoices for retail shoppers	
Thermal receipts difficult to store & lose print	Difficult to keep track of purchases & invoices	
Warranty cards et al maintained separately	Expense trackers require manual scanning & input	

Limited ability of retailers to maintain customer info

Limited communication from retailer to customer

High dependency on paper for invoices

Figure 9-2. *Emphasis on the challenges faced by retail customers and retailers on centralized platforms and offline processes*

As we can see, the conventional methods have multiple challenges related to storage, tracking, information capture, and expense management, to name a few for both the retailers as well as the shoppers. In order to overcome these, Bill'U uses a platform based out of AI and blockchains to ensure ease of service and customer data confidentiality.

Customer data confidentiality is one of the prime Unique Selling Points (USPs) of the product, as all of the alternates of this require the customer to furnish their personal information, like name, mobile number, and addresses, which is then used and over-used by retailers and has no clause around confidentiality of the data and further sharing of it.

In such scenarios, the customer ends up getting spammed instead of the information serving its intended purpose. Thus, Bill'U has been powered by a combination of public plus private blockchains that enable retailers to understand their customers' data and provides them with insights and relevant data, all while masking the personal data of the user. As the personal data is masked but the other relevant data is available on the public chain, the retailer can create custom offers for clients and use insights for the benefit of the clients, all while shielding the client's personal info, which is stored separately on the private chain of the hybrid blockchain, thus protecting the client's data and giving them a "wow" retail experience, which helps them take care of all relevant details after shopping.

The technical construct is shown in Figure 9-3.

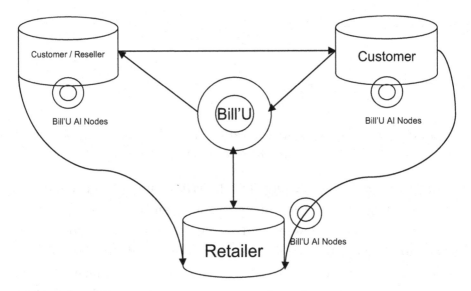

Figure 9-3. *Chain representation based on the transaction between users. Each user in a node has its own AI module to avoid sharing of private data*

Every user represents a peer node, whereas Bill'U performs the role of a validator node between billing transactions of documents between two stakeholders in a private chain. In the public chain, all peer nodes can derive trends, consumption demographics, and voucher offers from anonymous data distributed among all nodes. The AI processing of the Bill'U nodes is local to the user, which maintains the privacy of the most confidential documents on Bill'U. This prime feature of data security is rare to find in most AI applications, which compute on a server rather than on a device.

Here, the original data is kept secure as compared to the other AI services. The learnings from the nodes are on the public ledger, which do not expose the original data of users, thereby benefiting all stakeholders with recommended purchase trends and other recommendations with the Ask Bill'U service.

AI services being local to the user, Bill'U services are customer-centric. For example, when you use Ask Bill'U, it answers by learning from your data on your node and analyzing on the device itself. Meanwhile, Alexa or Siri go to some other server, taking all your data, analyze on the company server, and return back results that may or may not be biased.

Bill'U reminds the user about the expiry of warranties and prompts to use vouchers and birthday offers personal to the shopper. At the same time, it allows retailers to share bills wirelessly without any email or phone number dependency.

The querying mechanism for Ask Bill'U or the Make a Wish section, shown in Figure 9-4, is also local to the user. However, such a private service depends on the global learning of the AI module to understand the natural language of the user. Thus, when the service is catered through the blockchain ledger, the querying attempts to search locally on the node first, then traverses through the private ledger that is internally shared between the customer, retailers where this customer shops, the Bill'U global learning center, then, finally, the public ledger in the last case. This makes the response cover all aspects of the user in complete fairness.

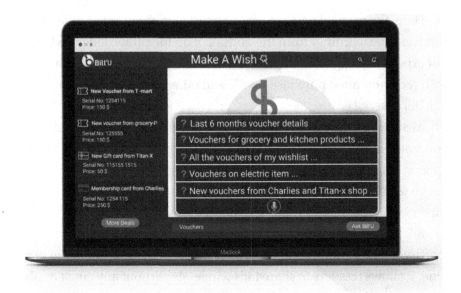

Figure 9-4. AI feature of Bill'U known as Make a Wish or Ask Bill'U that answers user's queries with respect to his bills

This detailed look at the AI capabilities is to understand the role of the blockchain on this platform. When such care is taken toward not exposing any confidential data while delivering AI services, the process of data transfer requires a careful choice of technology. Therefore, we utilize the encryption, decentralization, and transparency of the blockchain platform for the transfer of anonymous data on public blockchains exclusive to the users of the blockchain only, and send the personal transaction data between buyer and seller on the private chain. Any user outside the chain will have to join the ledger to access the public data, and if a user wishes to access a private blockchain, it will require the consensus of the stakeholders of the chain. Also, many times when confidential data is limited to an edge device, there is a risk of losing data due to physical damage, corrupt files, etc. Bill'U provides a private blockchain option for users to back up and replicate the node on another device or a virtual machine, thereby making it fault tolerant, secure, and accessible over the cloud, with distributed security on a private blockchain, where the participating nodes are the sole user accessing it from different devices.

Bill'U blockchain features:

- Digital vault for asset documents

- Digital locker for purchase documents

- Secure, encrypted, backed up personal ERP system

- Decentralized AI with global and local learning models

- Smart contract alerts for warranty expire, resale terms, etc.

- Universal billing format enabling smart contracts for resell, warranty, etc.

- Wireless bill-sharing platform without exposing your email, ID, or phone number (ref Figure 9-5, QR-based bill)

Figure 9-5. *Digitized bill on blockchains*

Since this platform is B2B2C, the blockchain architecture will be a hybrid network of public and private permissioned ledgers. The genesis node of Bill'U will be connected to all other retailers in the form of different decentralized networks. Bill'U will be connected to all types of vendors that can scan their bills and upload on the platform, which will digitize all types of receipts collected from the grocery shops, big department stores, medical offices, taxi drivers, even small merchandise, hospitals, restaurants, and movie tickets.

Each asset will be stored on the blockchain, since it is a private permissioned blockchain. Once the new block is updated on the ledger, no one can change the block on the ledger. Each transaction on the blockchain will be immutable.

The end user receives a unique hashed identifier formed with the private key, and only enabled parts of the public data can be viewed with the public key.

Using this unique identifier and private key, the end user can access his last expenses and get analytics and recommendations on top of it. However, this personal data remains anonymous with the unique hash ID.

This intermesh of chains with a common genesis, i.e., the Bill'U node, resembles several possible inter-chain architectures. One such architecture is formed by NTU's COMMENDO, which is a lightweight blockchain that forms the underlying chain of data and data processes.

Being a B2B2C platform, the expansive requirements of such a hybrid chain requires high-speed data transactions as well as scalability in terms of storage.

To enable several asynchronous transactions among various private chains and the flow of public data onto the public blockchain, the blockchain works over Apache Cassandra—a distributed database system. This ensures high availability and high read-write throughput. Bill'U's blockchain utilizes NTU's COMMENDO blockchain to allow anonymous transactions with distributed asynchronous worker queues.

Similarly, check out Azure's CosmosDB as a probable choice for a decentralized distributed database.

Azure CosmosDB is defined as Microsoft's globally distributed, fully decentralized, multi-mastered database service for mission-critical applications. It provides turnkey global distribution with multi-master replication, elastic scaling of throughput and storage worldwide, and single-digit millisecond write and read.

This is a major need of existing blockchains in terms of distributed large-scale storage.

To consider such a platform on an enterprise-grade ecosystem, it is crucial to identify a largely scalable database over a trustless and permissioned network. Consider Bill'U being used across enterprise businesses to store company bills, purchase orders, and so forth. Bill'U could track any changes made to the bills, purchase documents, and contracts. The interchain activities form a mesh of business nodes that form a consortium network.

The consortiums build shared applications on a blockchain to monitor the movement of those assets as they move across organizational trust boundaries and govern state changes with "on chain" logic in permissioned smart contracts. Use cases cover a range of scenarios that are asset- and workflow-centric, from claiming internal bills to tracking external purchase orders and contracts.

With such a secured end-to-end consortium of blockchains, the benefits of offers, vouchers, claims, resell, customer engagement, and customer satisfaction set up beautifully without compromising personal data.

While we see over here a very niche application that has been built with a combination of multiple emerging-tech softwares, let's look at an example that is closer to a conventional brick-and-mortar setup and has managed to employ blockchains to provide an unparalleled customer experience.

Microsoft Azure and Starbucks

Technology and life have always gone hand in hand. The technologists envision improving life with technology, and the life or the living beings are the ones to shape technology. This symbiotic relationship brings about the confluence of two companies—Microsoft Azure and Starbucks—to blend their experiences to make technology improve human lives.

Starbucks has been experimenting with cutting-edge technologies such as blockchain, AI, and IoT with Microsoft Azure to accelerate productivity, efficiency, and transparency and to provide an experience to the customers that is customized and highly personalized.

Microsoft CEO Satya Nadella at the 2019 Microsoft Build conference presented on how Starbucks is using emerging technologies to deliver its unique customer experience. In order to offer a more personalized experience for customers who visit Starbucks, the coffeehouse chain is using reinforcement learning technology that learns to make decisions in unpredictable environments based upon external feedback.

Customers receive custom-made order recommendations through the reinforcement-learning platform—developed and hosted in Microsoft

Azure—which helps them by suggesting things based on local store inventory, popular selections, weather, and time of day, community preferences, and previous orders.

If the demand and supply are in a closed loop, the profitability for the producer definitely increases on understanding the customers' demands. A cocoa farmer far away from the customer would gain understanding of the scale of growth, the type of cocoa to grow, and the seasonality of the demands. In reality, this information outreach is still not completely achieved. With the Azure Blockchain Services, the vision is to expand the inclusion of stakeholders, from farmers to consumers, in a closed loop.

Conversely, the technology can help boost demand in areas where it was untried before. For example, if there is a group of consumers who are known to like strong Columbian coffee, the recommendation engine for the blockchain public data could boost the recommendation of strong Jamaican coffee to these very users to help boost the demand for such fantastic farm coffee from Jamaica. This reinforcement learning algorithm reduces the chances of recommending unlikeable coffee to consumers on-chain, thereby generating a win-win in terms of outreach for the farmers as well as on the consumer end, as both are supported in terms of sales and experience, respectively.

The primary focus here is to bring greater financial possibilities for coffee farmers and allow the customers to track their coffee back to its source, making it experiential. This is said to be an ideal use case for Ethereum due to its transparent multiple individual nodes that verify transactions. Every involved party can freely track every single transaction made on Ethereum through Etherscan.

Note   Etherscan is a BlockExplorer for the Ethereum Blockchain. A BlockExplorer is basically a search engine that allows users to easily lookup, confirm and validate transactions that have taken place on the Ethereum Blockchain.

Starbucks envisions enhancing the consumer experience so they know the source of their coffee and have a direct understanding of its roots. At the same time, this process increases exposure to markets for the farmers.

For the effort, the coffee chain is working with Microsoft to harness its Azure Blockchain Service in tracking coffee shipments from across the world and bringing "digital, real-time traceability" to its supply chains, according to an announcement from Microsoft.

With the partnership, Microsoft's blockchain service will record all changes along the journey of the coffee on a shared ledger, providing participants with a "more complete view" of the supply chain.

The app will also inform consumers of how Starbucks is supporting these growers, Microsoft indicated.

This use case covers a very important aspect of **transparency** that blockchains provide (Figure 9-6).

Figure 9-6. *Stages of farm to cup for the coffee supply chain*

Note   Let us dig in deeper to analyze how the process might be broken down. As readers, one must try to correlate the use case with the technologies learned throughout the book. Remember: we are not reading facts and following them. We are inferring from the use cases to develop our solutions. Given the stage at which the technology is, one can always challenge with newer ways and constructs. So, let us break it down in a similar fashion and infer possibilities of implementations from understanding the use case.

Another important aspect of the use of blockchains is the automated efficiency and productivity they bring. Most of the time, in large enterprises and companies, the information flow of data reaches very late to the top management for effective direction. Even in the largest of the firms, the predictive approach is still not formulated, and digitization exists mainly in structured forms. Thus, Blockchains here enable digitization with credibility due to its immutable style of storage (add-only) & transparency across all processes involved. Thereby enabling the top management to drive data driven decisions based on the state of data/information across different timelines.

For example, consider a factory that does milling through hulling machinery for coffee. There is a small accident with one of the hulling machines. This issue goes unreported for a day. The next day, the supervisor realizes that the supply generated would be reduced by 1/10 due to the faulty machinery. The report goes to the management after ten days. The information flows down to the sales department sitting in another country on the fifteenth day. The customer on the end does not receive the order and cancels the order or charges a late fee.

This shows the impact of having transparency of data and unmonitored productivity rates. Now, for a company like Starbucks, with more than 30,000 stores worldwide serving 100 million customers a week, staying profitable irrespective of the seasonality, calamities, loss of productivity, and so on is of huge importance. At the same time, they don't want to reduce any experiential facilities for end customers.

Starbucks has integrated Azure Sphere—Microsoft's end-to-end solution for creating highly secure, connected devices—to deliver the following:

- **Hardware-based root of trust**: The device must have a unique, unforgeable identity that is inseparable from the hardware.

- **Small, trusted computing base**: Most of the device's software should be outside a small, trusted computing base, reducing the attack surface for security resources such as private keys.

- **Defense in depth**: Multiple layers of defense mean that even if one layer of security is breached, the device is still protected.

- **Compartmentalization**: Hardware-enforced barriers between software components prevent a breach in one from propagating to others.

- **Certificate-based authentication**: The device uses signed certificates to prove device identity and authenticity.

- **Renewable security**: Updated software is installed automatically, and devices that enter risky states are always brought into a secure state.

- **Failure reporting**: All device failures, which could be evidence of attacks, are reported to the manufacturer.

Imagine such MCU devices from Azure Sphere being embedded at every stage, from farm to cup. This would monitor the supply chain closely in a secure manner impermeable to hacks in an encrypted network of devices/nodes. At the same time, it would provide transparency and failure reporting to the proper stakeholders to increase predictability and manage costs accordingly (Figure 9-7).

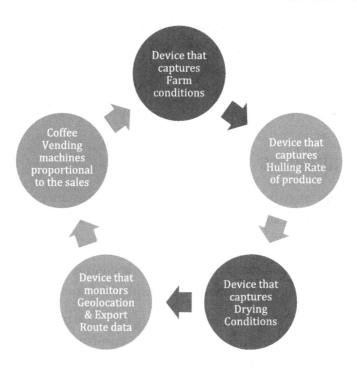

Figure 9-7. *An illustration of nodes that are IoT edge devices updating data to the blockchain*

The confluence of predictive models that run locally on these intelligent edge devices at every stage of coffee manufacturing so as to run the recommendation engine for the consumer makes it a complete closed loop supply chain, thus enhancing experiences for all involved. Having all of this connected on a blockchain makes traceability and accessibility highly transparent to the management of the company so they can make pro-active decisions in favor of most stakeholders. Decentralization here provides a promise to reduce losses and envisions opening up new avenues with its means of providing transparency and accessibility to farmers, customers, and business owners alike.

Last month, the Indian Commerce Ministry launched a blockchain-based coffee e-marketplace app that conducts transparent coffee trade in the country. The app is believed to bring a positive transformation among consumers who look for real Indian coffee, as well as for the grower who is paid fairly for the coffee produced.

Similarly, several economies are now gearing up to boost the efficiency of their supply chain with the confluence of AI, IOT, and blockchains, making it end-to-end digitized, tangible, and provable.

Other Industries

A couple more noteworthy use cases that deal with customer experiences in various industries are:

- The dairy industry, for which it is highly crucial to have transparency in terms of temperature control, shelf life of the product, conditions of transport and storage, etc.

- The health industry, where diet regimes have been a crazy fad across the social media. Many of us attempt to start and try various regimes without complete knowledge of our own bodies and the historical evidence of the diet. All that we have is a couple of internet searches and blogs telling us what to do. Visiting a dietician would surely be a credible source, as the time invested by the professional to understand your eating habits, regional differences, cultural impact, and medical history definitely would help.

  a. Here, technology could assist the accessibility of such a professional.

  b. Validate the data in terms of results on-chain with body monitors.

  c. IoT devices that update weight parameters on blockchain and trace the impact of various diet regimes.

However, how many of us would want to share our weight online at first? How is the privacy of an individual secured with technology to help us in certain ways? This is the difference between using a blockchain over a centralized internet platform. In the blockchain, which is decentralized, the authority distributed to the stakeholders regulates the activities of the chain in such a way that any activity might require the consensus of the entire chain. On an internet platform that is hosted by one single party, that party might have full authority to misuse your data and gain profits.

Therefore, a blockchain might be appropriate for such a use case, with IoT that connects people to validated dieticians, maintains anonymous shared blockchain data to trace the success rates of users, and incentivizes the customers rather than one company itself.

Decentralized Trade Finance

One of the most common and foremost use cases of blockchains came out of the challenges faced in the conventional operation of trade finance; a more direct case is the international trade finance, where changes in banks, banking regulations, and international trade laws create processes that cause it to take days for transactions to be closed.

Another challenge that comes up in such scenarios is the lack of transparency in terms of transfer of payments and the goods/services that have been provided in exchange and the sheer dependence on banks for the transaction (in most cases the bank of the other party may not even operate in your home country to offer assistance).

Other pain points that have been raised repeatedly are as follows:

- Error-prone manual processes for creating, validating, and auditing trade data and documentation

- Siloed data that is difficult to verify, leading to multiple versions of the truth and major fraud, compliance, and audit risks

- Disconnected legacy systems that limit new business opportunities and make it difficult for small and medium-sized businesses to gain access to financing alternatives

Therefore, as we have studied the impact on customer experiences of the refining of supply-chain procedures with blockchain technology in the last section, let us deep dive into the trade finance processes that impact life, trade., and our finances in this section.

Microsoft Azure and Banks

Microsoft News mentions that more than 80 percent of the world's largest banks are Azure customers.

To help solve the pain points mentioned under the "Decentralized Trade Finance" section, blockchains have been introduced and experimented with, and now are finally coming into mainstream use. Major players like Bank of America Merrill Lynch now called BofA Securities are taking the lead with Azure blockchains to create an ecosystem for trade finance that will be more transparent, and that too, as early as 2016, speaks volumes about the belief of the industry in the potential of blockchains. Banks like HSBC and ING Bank have followed suit, and the same phenomena is becoming popular across all financial institutions today.

To understand trade finance and the integration of blockchains better, let's look into the Bank Of America Merrill Lynch case in depth.

Microsoft and Bank of America Merrill Lynch announced a collaboration to use blockchain technology to fuel the transformation of trade finance transactions as early as 2016.

As part of this collaboration, the two companies decided to build and test technology, create frameworks, and establish best practices for blockchain-powered exchanges between businesses and their customers and banks. Microsoft Treasury experts served as the advisors and initial test clients, establishing the first Microsoft Azure–powered blockchain transaction between a major corporate treasury and a financial institution.

As we all know, when digitization started, there were many ERP systems that came into existence. With such software, the banks started increasing data entry to such systems, making it highly inefficient for people to support such a task, where the credibility of the data lay in the hands of the data-entry personnel. Not just in the banks, but all parts of trade finance—the importer, the exporter, the banks, the customs people, and other stakeholders—all had to fill in various kinds of paper and digital forms. This was highly manual, time consuming, and many times faulty. These systems used to store such data in plain-text, as most of them at the early stage of that technology were focused on simply aggregating data. However, the tamper-proof methods of storing such data were missing.

With blockchains, processes can be digitized and automated, transaction settlement times shortened, and business logic applied to related data, creating a host of potential benefits for businesses and financial institutions, including more predictable working capital, reduced counterparty risk, improved operational efficiency, and enhanced audit transparency, among other benefits, in a closed-loop network of anonymous transactions.

With this, blockchains open the door for streamlined trade finance, enabling participants to exchange data easily and track assets in real time. Microsoft is leveraging Corda, an enterprise-grade ledger that enables banks to limit who sees what information and selectively share data with only relevant parties. The solution involves blockchain technology paired with Azure and APIs, and could be used in the future to involve technologies like AI, machine learning, IoT, and more.

Upon using blockchains for the processing of letters of credit, the turnaround time for issuing an SBLC was reduced to three to five days from the earlier benchmark of three to five weeks! Similarly, the transaction settlement time for overseas transactions was reduced drastically after automating conditions on smart contracts. Once the conditions are fulfilled, the transactions are settled immediately.

With the blockchain encapsulating the challenge with validator nodes that actively validate the transaction, the settlement is made clear a lot faster. However, in the absence of a blockchain, the transfer of data requests for clearance are dependent on non-standardized processes, scattered systems, and so forth.

Microsoft further partnered with JP Morgan Bank to promote the Blockchain Service on Azure with the Quorum Blockchain. It enables the setup with a couple of clicks over Azure, integrating the Active Directory, event registers, and Visual Studio to write contracts and so forth. It applies all policies of the consortium defined by the Quorum Blockchain.

"In a rapidly globalizing digital world, business processes touch multiple organizations and great sums are spent managing workflows that cross trust boundaries. As digital transformation expands beyond the walls of one company and into processes shared with suppliers, partners, and customers, the importance of trust grows with it. Microsoft's goal is to help companies thrive in this new era of secure multi-party computation by delivering open, scalable platforms, and services that any company from game publishers and grain processors, to payments ISVs and global shippers can use to digitally transform the processes they share with others," explained Mark Russinovich, Chief Technology Officer, Microsoft Azure.

Other Financial Industries

Another set of applications that could benefit from a blockchain deployment of processes are the following:

- Decentralized KYC (Know Your Customer) and credit data validation

- Reduced risk of fraud and lower compliance costs

- New avenues of financing and tracing trade activities

As readers, one must question how the application is broken down into the real-life implementations. As we saw in the last chapter, the architecture for letters of credit involved an overseas trade activity.

Similarly, for these application use cases, let us speculate on the suitable tools, consensuses, and outcomes.

Decentralized KYC and Credit Data Validation

National and international governance bodies, such as the government, have been trying to standardize identity with the use of passports, biometric inclusions, Social Security numbers, and so forth. However, for financial institutions, the proof or onboarding of identity is usually a submission of non-standardized documents due to the diversity of cases of various individuals. Another dynamic to this situation is that during name changes or transfer of location, a lack of documents can cause great inconvenience to both parties—the financial institutions as well as the customer.

Here, the stakeholders of KYC are the prime customers and the businesses such as financial institutions that may transact with the customer. For any financial transaction, being it a bank account transaction, credit card transaction, deposits, or Mutual Funds (MFs), the bank needs to know the customer. This trust is established through the submission of authorized governmental documents or by referrals in some cases. However, the regulatory bodies that govern the safety of the financial economy require banks to spend time on regulation checks over KYC to avoid money laundering. Therefore, there is an increase in background checks, certificate authorization, and so on. Now imagine this check occurring on a blockchain network rather than in an offline process. In an offline process, a customer's data has to be passed from one party to another in a manner that is non-transparent to the end customer. This increases the risk of leak of confidential data, and at the same time such documents could be forged in known ways, making it difficult to trace such fraud. In the coming sections, we shall see how proof of identity is transformed on a blockchain, which could enhance KYC for trade finance, thereby improving internal processes to gain LoCs and bank guarantees.

Reduced Risk of Fraud and Lower Compliance Costs

Imagine a fully connected trade finance network in a particular location. All trade activities are digitized onto a blockchain, with every known entity on-chain. No off-chain activities are allowed to cross the borders without an update on this chain. In such an ideal case, the flow of transactions is tracked anonymously. However, in case of fraud within such a network where cash is laundered, the repeated illegal activity could be identified. Similarly, when any trade entity attempts to bypass the conventional methods of trade by finding a loophole, the chain records could identify such an outlier case. This makes it easier for regulatory bodies to enforce Anti Money Laundering (AML) and avoid a disbalance of the economy.

In the interest of forming a Global Trade Connectivity Network (GTCN), Hong Kong and Singapore's regulatory bodies—Hong Kong Monetary Authority (HKMA) and Monetary Authority of Singapore (MAS)—along with twenty banks collectively initiated digitization of trade flows for cross-border trade finance activities. Several other decentralized initiatives, with different banks forming consortiums, are We.Trade, Voltron, Trade Information Network, Marco Polo, BankChain, and more. All efforts are toward making data paperless and processes transparent and secure. From a technology standpoint, the pilot phases of several of these initiatives are still struggling with the choice of technology—whether to choose an enterprise close-sourced blockchain platform or an open-sourced blockchain platform. If one attempts to go enterprise, would the trust of the source code hosting the blockchain be blindly trusted by other stakeholders? Wouldn't an open-sourced hard fork of the platform version be more openly accepted? Does it allow interoperability and encourage more and more stakeholders to join such an ecosystem? Is the current task force ready to integrate the existing systems with such cutting-edge technology? These are the questions that are yet to be tried, tested, and explored for an entirely decentralized system.

As technologists, we could contribute logic apps for smart contracts, create effective node systems that connect on interchain networks, and educate our task force on adaptability to such open, decentralized platforms. As major financial institutions are invested in opening cross-border relations and policies, proofs of concept developed for any of these use cases would definitely gain traction if they genuinely solved a pain point. For example, one could create a fraud-detection tool that reviews anonymous data on the blockchain network and alerts the chain in case of any piggybacking of cash flow over an invalid trade. Such a tool could be included among the validator nodes. Similarly, auto checks of a smart contract could checklist the compliance of all documents required to conduct trade.

New Avenues of Financing and Tracing Trade Activities

With the advent of cryptocurrencies, many forms of tokenomics came into existence. Several retailers started accepting such modes of payment. Micro-lending and financing through such schemes became a possibility. However, due to the lack of regulation, the credibility of the tokens was many times not within the framework of a country. However, Bitcoin and Ethereum have managed to gain a lot of traction since Bitcoin's inception. With the micro-quantification of efforts and processes, incentivizing on-chain definitely provides advantages to the stakeholders.

Looking at another example that has been better enabled by blockchains, we will examine a leading organization that is a marketplace for the procurement of materials across the supply chain at the best prices across global markets. Ninety percent of world trade happens via the international shipping industry. Let us deep dive into the procurement cycles of the industry and how it is impacted by blockchain technology.

The Maritime Industry: Insurance, Procurement, and Trade

Let's look at one of the oldest industries, one that has existed from the time of the silk route—the maritime industry.

Given the scope of this industry, which spans the corners of the world, the large volume and large value of goods moved around, the large number of people employed, the complexities of the laws and regulations from every country, and the earlier discussed issue of trade finance, the use cases that can be improved with a blockchain-led intervention are numerous. Some of the cases that we can look into are as follows:

- Marine insurance

- Maritime marketplace

Marine Insurance

In 2017, one of The Big Four consultancies - EY along with Guardtime, a software security company announced the world's first blockchain platform for the field of marine insurance. The development and launch of this platform was a collaborative effort with A.P. Møller-Maersk A/S, ACORD, Microsoft, MS Amlin, Willis Towers Watson, and XL Catlin. The partners coming together for this went ahead with the move after a rigorous twenty-week POC.

The platform for this has been built on the Microsoft Azure global cloud technology and was the first of its kind in the insurance industry, and the phased rollout intends to cover end-to-end use across the marine industry.

The platform, based on a global platform, connects maritime clients, insurance brokers, insurance companies, and third parties to distributed common ledgers that help with the acquisition of data about identity, risk factors, and exposures. The same then integrates this information with insurance contracts. The platform can create and maintain asset data from multiple parties to link data to policy contracts; to receive and act upon information that results in a pricing or a business process change; to connect client assets, transactions, and payments; and to capture and validate up-to-date first notification or loss data.

An excerpt from the EY insurance leader Shaun Crawford lays out that:

Blockchain's potential to transform the insurance ecosystem has always been clear. What we have done is to move forward from potential to reality. This solution is the first to apply blockchain's transparency, security and standardization to marine insurance and is ready for commercial use. We look forward to deploying this technology across the marine insurance industry and are exploring how these findings and insights will be applied to other specialty insurance markets and beyond.

The platform deployed across the entire ecosystem of the marine insurance industry was built with the vision of addressing the challenges of its complex systems, which involve multiple parties, rules, duplication, and a lack of digital capture of data, along with issues with significant levels of reconciliation. The issues until then were causing problems with transparent access to data, linkage of data to the rest of the chain, and accuracy in underwriting risk by the insurance companies and the sharpening of their model with respect to the preceding issues.

The words of Lars Henneberg, the head of risk and insurance for
A.P. Møller-Maersk A/S in 2017, regarding this indicate that the problem
of risk comprehension and evaluation has an affinity or potential to be
addressed well by blockchains, thereby making the equation better for
everyone. In his words:

> *It is a priority for us to leverage technology to streamline and
> automate our interaction with the insurance market.
> Insurance transactions are currently far too tedious and fric-
> tional. The distance between risk and capital is simply too far.
> Blockchain technology has the potential to facilitate the
> desired development that is long overdue.*

Insurers can use this blockchain platform to improve their capital
and gain efficiencies, with increased transparency and reduced manual
data entry or reconciliation and administration costs. The platform has
been built over the Keyless Signature Infrastructure, also known as the KSI
platform.

Not just maritime, but all of the insurance industry can benefit from
blockchain technology, as it has the potential to bring in transparency,
remove time-taking activities, and reduce the cost at the same time. The
entire series of benefits make risk assessment sharper and more in real time.

If we go by the words of Mark Russinovich, Chief Technology Officer,
Microsoft Azure, we can see this:

> *Microsoft believes blockchain is a transformational technol-
> ogy with the ability to significantly reduce the friction of doing
> business, especially streamlining business processes shared
> across multiple organizations. Marine insurance is a prime
> example of a complex business process that can be optimized
> with blockchain. We remain committed to bringing block-
> chain to the enterprise, and are glad to work with EY,
> Guardtime and other industry experts to develop and deploy
> blockchain solutions powered by Microsoft Azure.*

As of now, blockchains are finding more and more use cases in the banking and financial services space owing to the ownership and transparency brought in by this technology. The initial example of trade finance has been picked up well, and now even lending, along with the insurance sector, is exploring the potential of blockchains.

Maritime Marketplace

Exploring another use case, one a little more on the technical side as we will explain the buildup of infrastructure and the flow of sequences, let's discuss the case of a marketplace for the maritime industry.

Like any other online marketplace that has completely changed our shopping habits, consumer behavior, and patterns involving spending money, the maritime marketplace has seen changes, but within the context and constraints of the ecosystem.

Unlike traditional blockchains, where all stakeholders are part of every transaction or validation on public ledgers, a hybrid chain of private and public ledgers would be suitable to run a maritime marketplace. On such a platform, one could purchase goods overseas, such as machinery, metals, chemicals, container ships, oil and gas, maintenance parts, and so on.

Decentralized ledger technology maintains the proof of transaction and traces the credibility of doing business and trade on-chain. Complying with the best trade practices on-chain enables high credit ratings due to on-time deliveries, timely fulfillment, and proper procurement procedures. Stakeholders may gain access to credit guarantees from banks involved in the trade finance of such an ecosystem.

The architecture was designed in such a way that all customers/ users of the ledger reside on the public chain (public to the company and its approved stakeholders only) to avail themselves of general listing information. The transactions between relevant stakeholders are conducted in a private chain.

The public ledger consensus works on Byzantine Fault Tolerance (BFT), whereas the private ledger is governed by the delegated proof of stake, where the initiator/block producers have a high stake through delegation and can share adequate stakes with other stakeholders of the transaction to conduct the business contract.

The contract state is stored on the private ledger, and the transaction directive is done through DAG (directed acyclic graph). This ensures that the transaction is super-fast and the storage is decentralized securely between only the relevant stakeholders.

The organization receives a graph view of all transactions across the hybrid chain instantaneously (Figure 9-8), thereby allowing it to delegate stakes so as to grant various access control rights to involved stakeholders.

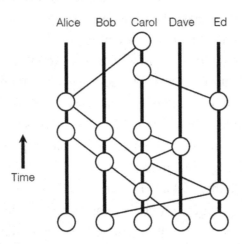

Figure 9-8. *Transactions on-chain: side chains*

Steps to develop such a marketplace via blockchains are shown in the following table. (Remember: As technologists and early adopters of blockchains, the cost to pilot them has to be minimalistic, since there is a cost of improvisation, education, and engagement for all stakeholders)

PROCESS	BLOCKCHAIN FEATURES
Foundation	• Hybrid chain—role based • Azure-based environments for fast deployments • BFT for public blockchains and PoS for private blockchains
Availability Check	• Ledger integration with POS • Decentralized ingestion of data • Validators and copy check • Distributed availability checker • Real-time, private chain creation based on availability and suitability
Order Process	• Smart contract generation • Transaction conditions based on contract status • Event registers for contract status • Smart contract trigger events • System alerts for smart contract stakeholders
Delivery Process	• Proof of work by document upload • Validators for confirmation • Auto-notification alert • MOSCORD auto checker by BFT • PO proof on immutable ledger
Invoice Process	• Platform invoice generator integration with smart contracts • Term translation and actions • Maintain copy on private ledger • Maintain validators
Payment Process	• ETH which is Ethereum's native currency transaction/ Hyperledger native currency value set up • Real-time financial transaction on private chain

Such a decentralized platform could enable a decentralized marketplace, where the policies are governed by the consensus of the validating stakeholders. The flow of onboarding stakeholders to the platform would be to add the aggregators of suppliers and their product offerings. The platform would enable direct peer-to-peer trade and also allow network-based trade, where the network regulates and validates the smart contract. This would enforce close control of fraudulent activities and reduce defaults. To design the smallest pilot, one should consider a private chain of one buyer and two suppliers, along with the set of regulatory nodes participating in the trade. Here, the block of data would be for the purchase of machinery parts, power tools, and safety items that are crucial for delivery. The trade deal on-chain would be initiated by a smart contract. If all on-chain activities fulfilled the conditions of the smart contract, it would quickly facilitate the payments. In the case of an incorrect supply delivery, the conditions of the smart contract would not trigger, and it would require the alternate clause of the smart contract to be executed. As developers of smart contracts, one must ensure all cases are covered. As solution architects, we must ensure the platform does not have any loopholes, and as business developers, defining such use cases is most crucial.

The patterns of fulfilling or defaulting on such smart contracts generate the credit risk valuation of the stakeholders, thereby allowing a fair valuation via a predictive approach that helps banks provide correct letters of credit and bank guarantees. This helps to reduce trade losses as well as fraudulent activities.

Document Signing and Record Management

Do you remember the last time you went to a bank? The foot traffic in bank branches has been reduced drastically with digitization.

Banks have come a long way since the time when there were only tellers, which were then replaced or re-allocated when the automated teller or the ATM came in, and now we have digital banks, which rest in our pockets in the form of applications and websites. Any transaction, irrespective of its value or volume, goes through with the same velocity and requires absolutely no paperwork.

One of the core things that enabled this, along with the technology, is the fact that people trust the tap of a button to handle their money as much as they earlier trusted a piece of paper. It's this trust—along with the plethora of benefits of digitization—that drove millions across the world, from a street vendor in India to a multi-billion-dollar fund manager in the United States, to move their banking online over a period of a few years.

Taking the premise of trust and digitization, let's look into another use case for blockchains, this time in the field of document signing and record management.

We are all aware of global processes like KYC (commonly known as Know Your Customer) or the on-boarding procedures at jobs that require us to furnish proof related to our identity or documents related to our education certificates, respectively. In all such processes, we are required to submit our digital documents—or physical ones, in some cases, even today. While it is understood that some of these cases might take a lot of time even after deploying AI-based parsers, the process of validation of documents is still fairly manual and time consuming, and this is not even the primary concern.

The major concern with using documents to ascertain the identity of a person or something like a college degree is that it is highly personal and prone to misuse, as in the case of a security breach. The recent case of Cambridge Analytica opened up to the world the extent to which data can be used and the impact it can have. Thus, it is imperative to have a solution for this that keeps trust, transparency, and security in the forefront.

Recognizing these factors, governments, banks, legal firms, courts, and even document storage companies are now building POCs that allow limited access, sharing, and authentication of document validation over a shared ledger.

A traditional platform that is centrally hosted usually asks its stakeholders or third-party engagements to simply comply with the platform without any promise or means to maintain the security of the data. For example, while uploading scanned documents of identity, one is asked to attest to the physical signature and upload the scanned copy, and then it is verified manually even today.

Let's consider a case where service providers are asked to sign an invoice to raise the bill of service (Figure 9-9).

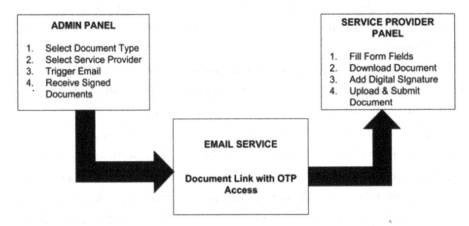

Figure 9-9. *A normally hosted service platform*

In such a system, there is no attempt to reach consensus or provide a platform for such an option. It is a straightforward, single-focused platform. Similarly, in the education field our degree certificates are signed by the central authority of the education board.

During background checks, one of the most expensive processes is to trace the truth of the source and physically check its existence in their records. Now, when the data is collated on a single blockchain network of truth and trust where all—the source as well as the end destination nodes—exist, the blocks of data transmitted in encrypted formats ensure the data request is witnessed and that a fraudulent request may not occur in the first place. In simple words, consider a real use case where all educational certificates (data blocks) lie on the shared ledger, and where the university is the source node and the companies that require validation are the end destination nodes. The student/employee nodes initiate the validation request on-chain and get verified over the shared ledger. In such systems, a student may never be able to fake a certificate as the witness of the source is on-chain.

Another important aspect of using digital signatures for documents is that it leaves a machine fingerprint in the form of the address of the node. Therefore, such digital traces cannot be forged, and it is difficult to develop fakes.

In a smart contract that formulates the consensus of a chain, the digital signatures of documents would simply be the machine address captured upon accepting the conditions of the smart contract. Not all digital signatures are developed purely from the machine address, however. Many times it is a mathematical formula that encapsulates the hash address of the node along with the private key.

With such a valid digital signature for a document on the ledger, one would not be able to retract the signed block, thus embedding trust of the true source of the signature (authenticity) and ensuring no alteration of the data transmission.

To understand the role of digital signatures, we will consider an industrial use case of art blockchains—a decentralized ledger that stores and transmits the state of the artwork (block) from the artist to the art buyer (refer to Figure 9-10).

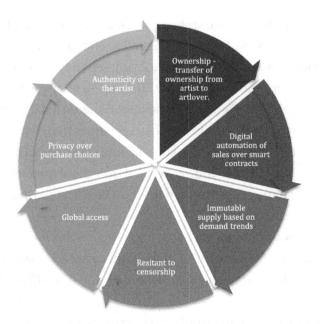

Figure 9-10. *Actions taken over blockchain with respect to the artworks as assets*

The clear advantages of using blockchains in document management and signatures are as follows:

- Cost savings – This is the most obvious benefit. Because blockchain transactions don't require intermediaries, processes can be made more efficient and less expensive. There's no need for auditors or legal professionals to validate the authenticity of information, so those costs come out of the process.

- Efficiency – Fewer people means faster turnaround. Transactions that might take days waiting for multiple sign-offs can be concluded in seconds.

- Security – The fewer participants there are in a transaction, the less risk there is that something could go wrong. Handoff points are a prime vulnerability, and blockchains effectively eliminate them.

- Flexibility – Any digital asset can use a blockchain, including difficult-to-protect items like multimedia and email records.

Source: Iron Mountain

As we learn the extent of the applicability of blockchain technology and its advantages over traditional methods, we are going to look into another application that has been brought to the world by an organization that was once a giant in the field of photography and related devices and accessories and then picked up again with a pivot into tech with blockchain. The organization under discussion here is none other than Kodak.

The recent pivot of Kodak to blockchain has been on the public stage since Kodak's announcement that it would build a new blockchain-based document management system. The service developed by the company does not depend on a third-party license and is completely developed and owned by Kodak.

Kodak Services for Business, as the suite is called, is a platform built with the aim to store and manage documents that are sensitive in nature in an efficient and secure manner. The Kodak Document Management Platform is intended to provide businesses and governments a facility to handle documents by storing them with security and regulating access over a blockchain.

Kodak estimates a 20 to 40 percent cost savings through the automation of workflows and decrease in human intervention in content, information, and documents. In January 2018, a third party licensed the Kodak brand name for KODAKCoin, which was designed to work with a blockchain developed to track image copyrights online.

Similar to how the supply chain was one of the foremost reasons for blockchains to scale up, the process of document management and security is becoming more popular in the blockchain space. It is not only Kodak that is looking at it as a potential offering to businesses.

Billon, a Polish-British fintech firm, is also working on a platform for a blockchain-based document management system.

The digitization of documents in the digital era, given the redundancy and reconciliation efforts wasted in hard copy, has driven companies to look into digitization and further builds a case for blockchains as the most viable option, considering security and access control.

With this, we come to the end of the part of the book where we reflect upon use cases and technical learnings. We envision helping you to evaluate your understandings and learnings in the next chapter. Chapter 10 further provides hands-on exercises.

CHAPTER 10

Puzzles and Exercises

This chapter helps to validate the learning curve over Blockchains and enables to design blockchain implementations. Attempt the challenges presented here hands-on to develop your skill. Refer back to the chapters relevant to the question. As the vision of this book is to enable readers from technical as well as non-technical backgrounds to be a part of the blockchain ecosystem, attempting this chapter is one of the validators as well as a catalyst to innovate further.

The exercises cover the following:

- Terminology

- Consensus algorithms

- Design challenges

- Blockchain or not?

- IoT with blockchain

- Smart contracts

- Mind maps

Remember: These exercises may have more than one correct answer. Also, as this is a field of innovation, the facts may evolve to a different form of existence. However, the fundamentals of decentralization, transparency, encryption, and immutability will remain the same. One may reflect upon the past chapters in different ways on every iteration of study.

© Shilpa Karkeraa 2020
S. Karkeraa, *Unlocking Blockchain on Azure*,
https://doi.org/10.1007/978-1-4842-5043-3_10

Throughout the book, we have examined various use cases across different industries. Before you start the exercises, choose one of the roles and view the challenges from that user's lens.

For example, if you read this book as a business developer, look at the infrastructure impact around the platform, the kind of people to interact with on-chain, and the policies that will have to be formed off-chain as well as on-chain. The challenges with respect to design will help you identify the right stakeholders to facilitate such a decentralized ecosystem.

If you read as a solution architect, draw out the variables internal to the platform. Analyze the changes in these variables. Focus on the pros and cons of each variable from your standpoint. Identify various technology stack options for every use case and its maturity for each use case.

If you read as a developer, focus on the tangibility of existing solutions with respect to the problem definitions at hand. To ensure building capabilities for better consensus algorithms and smart contracts, practice flow charts of execution, pseudo codes of business conditions, and user stories, and finally form it in the code. This code syntax may evolve from platform to platform; however, the fundamental logic will remain the same.

Attempt these challenges with the focus and vision that you are working for. If you are working in a team comprising a business developer, a solution architect, and a developer, the book encourages you to solve the challenges individually and exchange notes to have a broader understanding from different perspectives and roles.

Solutions are provided at the end of the chapter.

Getting Terminologies and Definitions Right

Crossword 1

Across

1. A digital agreement stored on the blockchain
2. adding transaction records to the blockchain ledger
3. _____ are distributed computers in the network that all have a copy of the entire blockchain

Down

1. public digital ledger of past transactions in order
2. first decentralized cryptocurrency
3. In blockchain transactions are combined into single _____
4. Smart contract language
5. Hash–based data structure
6. A long string of alphanumeric characters used to send, receive, or hold currency.

Crossword 2

Across

1. Entities that have stake in a transaction
2. Nodes that participate in consensus
3. Collection of information coded for further processing

Down

1. _____ Block - first block of a blockchain
2. Smart contract language
3. Public blockchains
4. A consensus algorithm
5. method of secure storage & transfer of data by converting with mathematical principles
6. Public blockchains

Crossword 3

Across

1. delegated away from center
2. Proof of Importance
3. Federated Byzantine Agreement

Down

1. A process of making a service available
2. Essential aspect for organization
3. Public blockchains
4. XRP Ledger Consensus Protocol
5. agreement among a group of people

Crossword 4

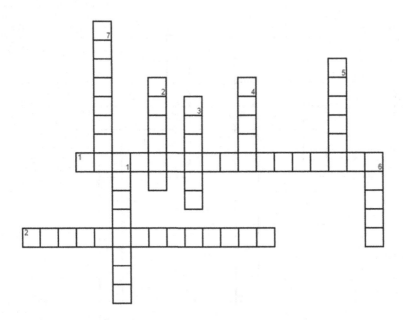

Across

1. blockchain framework implementation
2. digital or virtual currency that uses cryptography for security

Down

1. set of rules
2. Public blockchains
3. Valuing the chain & its utility to stakeholders
4. Cloud service provider
5. principle book of records
6. Public blockchains - transparent music streaming digital payments
7. Smart contract language

Choose the Suitable Form of Consensus

Match the three columns of consensus, blockchain, and features by drawing lines and linking the correct trio.

Consensus Mechanisms	Blockchain Platform	Features
1. Proof of Work	a. NEM	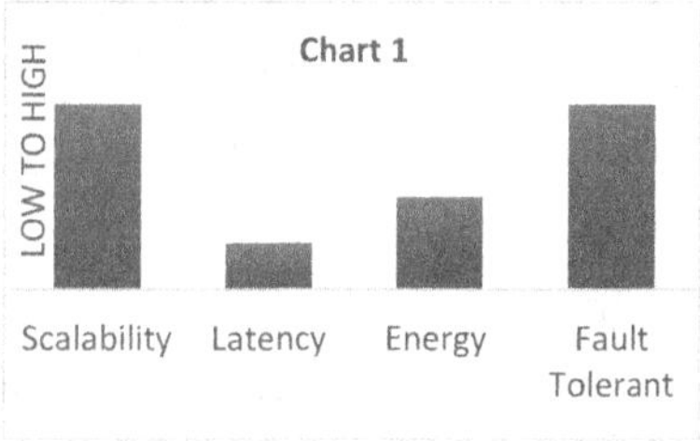
2. Proof of Importance	b. EOS	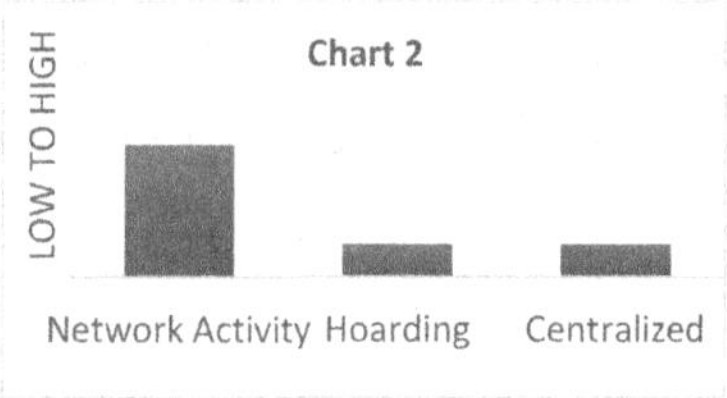
3. Federated Byzantine Agreement	c. Ethereum	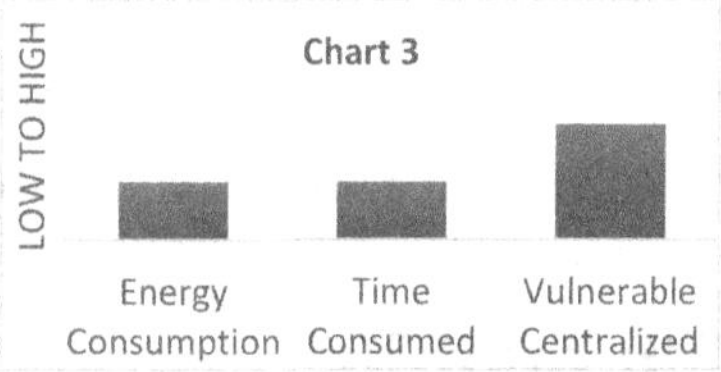
4. Delegated Proof of Stake	d. Stellar	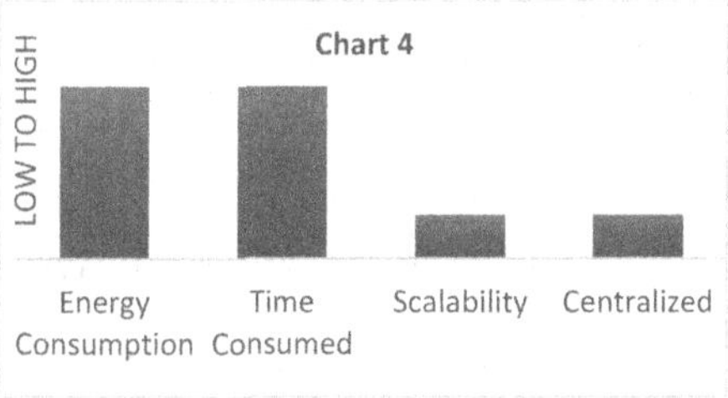

Chart 1

LOW TO HIGH

Scalability   Latency   Energy   Fault Tolerant

Chart 2

LOW TO HIGH

Network Activity   Hoarding   Centralized

Chart 3

LOW TO HIGH

Energy Consumption   Time Consumed   Vulnerable Centralized

Chart 4

LOW TO HIGH

Energy Consumption   Time Consumed   Scalability   Centralized

Use Case Design Challenge

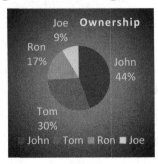

A farm of one acre is purchased by four friends in the percentage of stake as shown in the pie chart.

They agree to run a farming business together on the land. John does not live close to the land, thereby would not be around to work on it; he wants to rent or sell parts of the land. Tom has a full-time job and will work after his working hours. Ron lives beside the farm, but has no knowledge of farming. Joe is fully available to work on the farm as well and has complete knowledge and experience.

They decide to gain consensus of all involved to make every decision. Therefore, you have to design a blockchain platform for all activities that are going to be conducted on-chain. In the following sections, write the advantages and drawbacks of each type of consensus for its suitability to this situation. List the activities that can work under each type of consensus.

Example Solution

Proof of Work

Activities on-chain:

- Land registry and underwritings

- Ownership and sectoring of land

- Adding users on submission of documents and validation by peers

- Request for join budgets and cost claims on upload of receipts such as property tax, electricity, and water

- Profit share can be initiated when revenue crosses 2x of investments as per smart contract

Advantages:

- On-chain decisions have tamper-proof records of all activities for new users to preview.

- Paper trail of all transactions can be found on-chain.

Limitations:

- John cannot sell the land to any random user till he has all the conditions of the smart contract fulfilled and validated by peers.

- Tom, who works after hours for the farm, does not get profit-share returns until the consensus clause is fulfilled.

- Ron wants to expand his courtyard for parties and weddings but cannot do so until validation across the chain is met.

- Joe, who works full time, wishes to hire more people on the farm but cannot do so until he gains validation from all.

Now that we have evaluated one form of consensus for this set of activities, list out activities and their suitability to the mentioned form of consensus. Remember, as a part of studying, developing, and forming blockchains, one is free to design as required with the choice best suited to the scenario.

Proof of Stake

Activities using this form of consensus are purely based on the stake of ownership in the unsectored land. It requires the block proposer to gain validation from the high-stake holders through the voting mechanism based on the weight of stakes.

If validator nodes based on their weight form the majority, the block transaction is allowed.

For example:

```
If
W1 x1 + W2 x2 + W3 x3 + W4 x4 + W5 x5 > 60%
then
```

```
        Allow block transaction activities
```

where weights are proportional to the actual stakes.

Activities on-chain:

-
-
-
-
-

Advantages:

-
-
-
-
-

Limitations:

-
-
-
-
-

Delegated Proof of Stake

This consensus algorithm tries to decentralize further from PoS to enable a fairer voting mechanism. The algorithm delegates and reassigns weights for various activities at random. This can be pre-defined or chosen at random or delegated every cycle by the owner of stake.

Activities on-chain:

-
-
-
-
-

Advantages:

-
-
-
-
-

Limitations:

-
-
-
-
-

Directed Acyclic Graphs (DAG)

In the traditional forms of consensus observed in Bitcoin and Ethereum blockchains, the scalability and the latency time have been of increasing concern with the increase of their popularity and adoption. Therefore Directed Acyclic Graphs, a well-known graph data structure, can provide a method for a common consensus policy to maintain the shared ledger in a acyclic, low-latency, non-mining-dependent, pruned, lightweight-transactions manner on-chain.

Several blockchains generate variants of DAG based on the activity on-chain. For example, if there are 25 retailers on-chain selling different items in different sectors with entirely unique customer profiles, the blockchain ledger could be a DAG, where each transaction entry for every retailer is independent of the other retailers. This could be viewed as a side-chain activity that runs in a silo. However, the data needs to be tamper-proof, locked onto a decentralized chain.

Activities on-chain:

-
-
-
-
-

Advantages:

-
-
-
-
-

Limitations:

-
-
-
-
-

Federated Byzantine Agreement (FBA)

Remember: John is not always online to be involved in all activities for the farm. However, the group wants to ensure fair decisions that are transparent and agreeable to the chain node members. John, being a major stakeholder, becomes a bottleneck validator in the case of other mechanisms of consensus. FBA provides a fault-tolerant method to validate transactions on-chain. Identify the activities that require such a mechanism.

Activities on-chain:

-
-
-
-

Advantages:

-
-
-
-
-

Limitations:

-
-
-
-
-

Proof of Importance

Importance could be a metric on-chain over which decisions can be made. For example, a real-time surgery in a hospital might be of higher importance than a dental check-up; therefore the hospital policies for these scenarios are graded accordingly. Similarly, in this use case of farmland, a hazardous situation in the field might require faster decision-making. Or the most active member on-chain might get the authority to validate the transaction. So, this mechanism is not merely limited to the definition by NEM, but may be defined as required.

After defining the activities and node types, analyze the suitable token mechanics to govern the laws of the chain.

For example, NEM is defined at the following:

https://nem.io/wp-content/themes/nem/files/NEM_techRef.pdf

Similarly, one can define their own scoring formulae.

Activities on-chain:

-
-
-
-
-

Advantages:

-
-
-
-
-

Limitations:

-
-
-
-

Note that the consensus might not be a single mechanism but rather a synergistic design of methods that enforce a common policy across the chain to provide attack resistance and asynchronous race conditions.

Now we have considered different scenarios with different forms of consensus. One can always build a hybrid network of blockchains for different purposes with different types of users. For example, a simple landowner registry might not require consensus validation from every node and may be relevant to just the owner if the land is entirely independent. However, if it is shared land, one can choose to agree on a common consensus for various activities on a traceable ledger of records of every action.

Hybrid Chain

Such a blockchain maintains high transparency for all involved as well as allows prospective buyers to have a single source of shared truth.

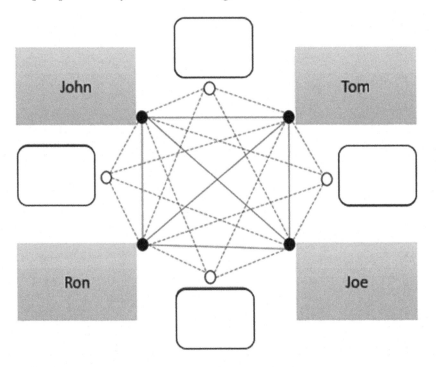

● Private ○ Public

Your task is to fill in the public nodes in the above hybrid chain for the landowner registry use case.

Data and Transactions

The city of Xoroville has agreed to maintain all health records and medical activities. Your job is to list the data and transactions that occur on the public chain and on the private chain.

Public Chain		Private Chain	
	Transaction		Transaction
Data	Activity	Data	Activity

Energy Allocation

Energy allocation inside a huge plant of 25 factories requires a blockchain to enable a shared ledger of data to trace electricity requirements.

Debate using the tools provided in the book whether a blockchain is required or not. Identify the exact circumstances where it is truly required.

Required	Not Required

Now that you have identified the exact case where it is required, identify the peer nodes that are required to be on-chain and off-chain.

Note   Peer nodes may or may not be end users. They can be users, machinery, sensors, and so forth.

On-Chain Entities	Off-Chain Entities

Gadgets

Two questions about gadgets:

- Identify five gadgets around you that need to be in consensus to work.

- Identify five gadgets around you that need to be in consensus to work for a chemical factory.

Transparent Updates and Fair Trade

Identify a use case where IoT, blockchains, and human interventions can form a decentralzied ecosystem of transparent updates and fair trade with smart contracts.

Having understood the design thought process for IoT integrations with blockchain, one can structure the platform with Azure components. Azure provides an array of options to configure the choice of blockchain with its workbench to connect with IoT devices along with other logic apps.

Depending on the design architected, one can decide to invoke the blockchain based on the integrations and the pre-defined conditions. For example, every time the sensor crosses a threshold, the blockchain would want to record it for audit purposes. So, when the sensor data crosses the threshold, the API to the blockchain is called. The DLT services ensure the hashing and generation of blocks is processed on the piece of data and it is added to the blockchain ledger.

However, it must be made clear that for a direct monitoring and alarm system that connects to the IoT, a blockchain may not be required. Therefore the Power BI can directly be connected to the off-chain DB as shown. The purpose of the blockchain ledger would be to maintain immutable records, enable an audit to trace all states of the sensory data, to ensure consensus is maintained in a forwarding system dependent on the sensory data, and so on.

One such example could be oxygen cylinders' sensor data that may be connected to life support, incubation centers, child care, and so on. With a requirement to maintain such information for hospital audits, such sensor data can be stored on this tamper-proof blockchain ledger, which is linked to a chain of devices. The level of supply can be continuously checked for its state at all nodes.

JSON Preparation

Create the JSON config pseudo code and the state diagram for the following use case: the blockchain platform captures every state and state change that occurs while invoking the smart contract conditions. Learning from the official smart contract flow for a wheel-alignment system, observe the JSON preparation steps:

1. Define the user types.

2. Define the states.

3. Draw the processes/steps to the ideal condition.

4. Decide the states on user activity.

Fixing Pain Points

In this section, let us examine existing off-chain scenarios and their drawbacks. As solution architects, fix the pain points identified with the blockchain solutions in the following image.

The elements of this supply chain are highly disconnected from each other as far as understanding the supply demand in terms of cost of inventory, stocking, and runout. This is because the communication between all stakeholders is limited and there is zero transparency of the end user's order. Most of these small-scale entities predict the demand flow in a silo, causing costs when not computed based on the entire chain's movements.

To understand more, play the game here: `https://beergame.masystem.se/`

Now that we understand the off-chain problem, design an entire blockchain solution with the following steps:

1. Choose stakeholders and roles.

2. Choose the blockchain configuration and linkages.

3. Choose the consensus type.

4. Choose the platform based on Step 3.

5. Measure the scalability requirements.

6. Define the token economics if required.

7. Set up the states and conditions of the smart contracts.

8. Draw the chain view of the consortium blockchain.

So, now that you have learned to choose the correct form of consensus for a real-life scenario, identified off-chain and on-chain activities, and selected the right set of peer nodes, validator nodes, and blockchain configuration in the consortium, let's see the solutions in the following sections.

Solutions

Crossword 1

Across

1. smartcontract
2. mining
3. nodes

Down

1. blockchain
2. bitcoin
3. block
4. kotlin
5. merkletree
6. address

Crossword 2

Across

1. stakeholders
2. validator
3. data

Down

1. genesis
2. rideon
3. minds
4. proofofwork
5. cryptography
6. litecoin

287

Crossword 3

Across

1. decentralized
2. nem
3. stellar

Down

1. distribution
2. security
3. ethereum
4. ripple
5. consensus

Crossword 4

Across

1. hyperledgerfabric
2. cryptocurrency

Down

1. protocol
2. monero
3. tokens
4. azure
5. ledger
6. choon
7. solidity

Matched Ordering Sequence

1 – C – Chart 4

2 – A – Chart 2

3 – D – Chart 1

4 – B – Chart 3

Proof of Stake Design Challenge

Activities on chain:

- Sale/lease of the land

- Addition of new stakeholders

- Approval of budget proposals

- Allocation of funds

- Immovable asset building

Advantages:

- Control among high-stake holders

- Chance to gather together to form majority even for a small stakeholder

- Raise proposal requests on chain transparently

- Track fund allocations based on consensus

- Transparent investment decisions

Limitations:

- Low control for minority voters and stakeholders

- Concentrated power by a group of nodes

- Rigidity and influence of majority stakeholders

- No avenue for decision-making for very low-stake holder groups

- Cannot be expanded to other users, third parties who do not have a stake to be a part of any decision-making or services on chain

By understanding the advantages and disadvantages of the methods of PoW and PoS, existing blockchain networks like Ethereum are now migrating to the hybrid model of PoW/PoS. One may decide to formulate PoW for a set of activities such as block creation and generation; and PoS to validate and approve as per smart contracts. This confluence of methods might help to eliminate disadvantages such as attacks, biases, and so on. Study the latest Ethereum Yellow Paper here:

```
https://ethereum.github.io/yellowpaper/paper.pdf
```

On studying the yellow paper, one could construct such a blockchain configuration either with the Azure Workbench or simply by utilizing a group of Ubuntu servers on Azure, with emulation of the nodes done through the docker files. Each server may be a node or a group of nodes on the virtual instances inside a server. Once the role allocation of the server allocation is clear, the user can connect the end points of each server to the event register, which can invoke the smart contract on top of it.

Delegated Proof of Stake

Activities on chain:

- Nomination of stake responsibility

- Task allocation and ownership

- Inclusion of third-party nodes, users, services

- Delegation to new farming professionals to work actively on behalf of stake owner

- Tenants on farm may be delegated some stake for certain activities

Advantages:

- Shared decentralized balanced forms of responsibility

- Avenue for low-stake holders to gain delegated stakes for various transactions/activity

- Failsafe method to avoid concentration of power based on pre-defined stakes

- Inclusion of new nodes can be onboarded based on random consensus of on-chain delegated nodes.

- Allows expansion of on-chain activities with decentralization and inclusion

- Low energy consumption

- Low latency periods

Limitations:

- Vulnerable to centralization and biases

- Fake consensus by delegated nodes to create false transaction, which may not be in the best interests of the original stakeholder

- Exclusion of non-delegated stakeholders

One example of a variant of Proof of Stake is Harmony. Harmony enables an adaptive threshold mechanism for various stake requirements for various activities. Nodes that qualify for the value of stake may participate. Harmony maintains its scalability and decentralization by sharding the network, data, and the states of transaction entirely. The sharding mechanism is non-uniform, scalable, and secure throughout. The consensus combines the Adaptive PoS with FBFT (Fast Byzantine Fault Tolerance), making it fault tolerant, distributed, and able to support high-speed transactions.

Directed Acyclic Graphs (DAG)

Activities:

1. Daily video feeds of the farms

2. Sensor based IoT feeds

3. Internal micro-transactions between Joe and Ron

4. Localized validations

5. Easily expandable to other nodes external to the core stakeholders for activities such as plumbing, electricity, notarization, etc.

6. Export of farming produce

7. Import and inventory management of seeds, farming material, etc.

8. Third-party integration triggers for security, fire hazards, etc.

Advantages:

1. Validation responsibility is a natural progression by later block producers.

2. Shared ledger information management does not require manual validation every time, thereby allowing IoT data to be appended to the immutable ledger seamlessly.

3. Allows offline status of nodes for transactions that may be irrelevant to someone like John and still maintains records for later awareness for such stakeholders.

4. Allows high-speed data transmission

Disadvantages

1. Disconnect from snoozed nodes

2. A one-way street of data ingestion and validation

3. Vulnerable to attacks

4. Prone to centralization

Federated Byzantine Agreement

Activities:

1. Approval for micro-budget transactions

2. Addition of family nominees or trusted known node users

3. Fixing of maintenance items on-field

4. Upload of bills and receipts

5. Regular activities on-field

Advantages:

1. Highly fault tolerant

2. Enables faster decision-making

3. Allows transactions

4. Allows non-trivial information to be added with curated validation of random nodes

Disadvantages:

1. Suited only for a certain set of activities that are limited to non-trivial decisions

2. Fault tolerance assumes bypassing crucial node members is fine

Proof of Importance

John, Ron, Tom, and Joe decide to rank all the preceding listed activities and decide that based on the work they do, importance scores will be earned on-chain. For example, John ensured all paperwork regarding the land was perfect and was uploaded on the ledger. So, apart from being a high-stake holder of land, he contributed to crucial activities, incentivizing him on-chain. Similarly, others are enabled to complete tasks and gain importance. However, a high importance score holder can allow the next task assignment. The scores are reviewed every seven days, and the validators shift based on the score. This is the agreement that was locked in under Proof of Importance.

Activities:

1. Incentivizing employees for contributions and actions

2. Incentivizing third-party entities that interact with this chain

3. Incentivizing a highly active member who works for the farm

4. Linkage of performance to importance

Advantage:

1. Provides an avenue for a low-stake holder like Joe to gain importance as well as value based on his contribution

2. Allows shift of authority based on engagement and involvement

Disadvantage:

1. Hoarding of power, value generated on chain

2. High dependency on network-driven activities

3. Decentralization may cause complete loss of control in some situations where governance is required.

4. May require revision or a hard fork to change policies

Hybrid Chain

Such a Blockchain maintains high transparency for all involved as well as allows prospective buyers to have a single source of shared truth.

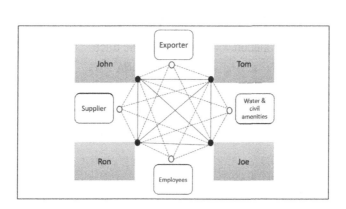

Data and Transactions

Public Chain		Private Chain	
Data	**Transaction Activity**	**Data**	**Transaction Activity**
General demographics	Pathology lab audits	Detailed blood reports	Doctor patient transactions
BMI	Hospital inspection checks	Surgery records	Hospital patient transactions
Anonymous Names	Doctor education and work experience history	Therapy session details	Pharmacy patient transactions
Area of Diagnostics	Purchase of general medical items	Family history	Insurance claim transactions
Blood Group	Purchase of medical instruments and quality	X-rays, sonography	Financial transactions
General Blood Reports	Blood donation	Genetic trace and DNA	
Doctors Records	Organ donation with anonymous donors	Biometrics	
Hospital Records			
Insurance Certificates			

Energy Allocation

Required	Not Required
When one factory proportionately increases or decreases consumption for other 24 based on its operations.	When 25 factories have no dependency on each other over electricity consumption.
When Smart Meters are everywhere and data can be integrated seamlessly	When this data is populated purely by manual intervention and meter readings
When this data affects the costs of the produce, must be highly sensitive.	When this data does not affect overall operations and the requirements are highly stable every year.

On-Chain Entities	Off-Chain Entities
Records of electricity consumption data from Smart Meters	Aggregation of one-time data of machinery that are not connected to the main line, but use batteries
Operation managers, which manage the electricity usage	Forecast of further electricity consumption
Bill invoices to 25 factories	M&A of factories
Disbursement and payments of bills	Faulty meter checks
Transfer of stakeholders	

Gadgets

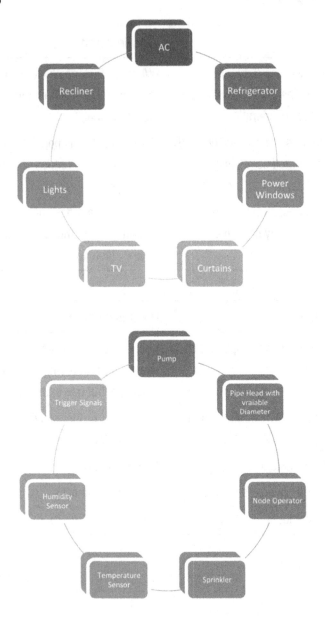

Transparent Updates and Fair Trade

Consider a scenario where organs for transplant have to be transported. The hospital patient who subscribes to the service as well as the doctor gets to see the quality of the transfer throughout the transport.

The blockchain ledger can have the following nodes:

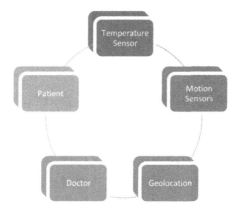

This private chain has a bound smart contract that has all conditions of a proper transplant requirement. If the IOT nodes satisfy, it finally requires the doctor's on-chain signature along with the patient's multi-sign on the acknowledgment. This permissioned chain enables a transparent process that may be tamper-proof on a decentralized system. Therefore, blockchains here make ideal sense.

JSON Preparation

```
{
  "ApplicationName": "WheelalignmentCheck",
  "DisplayName": "Service Contract for Wheel Alignment",
  "Description": "...",
  "ApplicationRoles": [
    {
```

```
    "Name": "Technician",
    "Description": "Contractor who aligns the wheel."
  },
  {
    "Name": "Car Owner",
    "Description": "Requests for Service"
  }
],
"Workflows": [
  {
    "Name": "Wheel Alignment",
    "DisplayName": "Wheel Alignment",
    "Description": "...",
    "Initiators": [ "Technician" ],
    "StartState":  "Created",
    "Properties": [
      {
        "Name": "State",
        "DisplayName": "State",
        "Description": "Holds the state of the contract",
        "Type": {
          "Name": "state"
        }
      },
      {
        "Name": "Technician",
        "DisplayName": "Technician",
        "Description": "...",
        "Type": {
          "Name": "Technician"
        }
      },
```

```
  {
    "Name": "Car Owner",
    "DisplayName": "Car Owner",
    "Description": "...",
    "Type": {
      "Name": "Car Owner"
    }
  },
  {
    "Name": "Target Wheel Angle",
    "DisplayName": "Target Wheel Angle",
    "Description": "...",
    "Type": {
      "Name": "int"
    }
  },
  {
    "Name": "Mode",
    "DisplayName": "System Mode",
    "Description": "...",
    "Type": {
      "Name": "enum",
      "EnumValues": ["Misaligned", "Aligned", "Not mounted"]
    }
  }
],
"Constructor": {
        "Parameters": [
            {
                "Name": "WA Technician",
                "Description": "...",
                "DisplayName": "Technician",
```

```
                        "Type": {
                          "Name": "Technician"
                        }
                },
                {
                        "Name": "WA Car Owner",
                        "Description": "...",
                        "DisplayName": "Car Owner",
                        "Type": {
                          "Name": "Car Owner"
                        }
                }
            ]
    },
      "Functions": [
      {
        "Name": "Start Wheel Alignment",
        "DisplayName": "Start Wheel Alignment"",
        "Description": "...",
        "Parameters": []
      },
      {
        "Name": "Set Wheel Angle",
        "DisplayName": "Set Wheel Angle",
        "Description": "...",
        "Parameters": [
          {
            "Name": "target",
            "Description": "...",
            "DisplayName": "Target Wheel Angle",
            "Type": {
```

```
        "Name": "int"
      }
    }
  ]
},
        {
  "Name": "SetMode",
  "DisplayName": "Set Mode",
  "Description": "...",
  "Parameters": [
    {
      "Name": "mode",
      "Description": "...",
      "DisplayName": "Mode",
      "Type": {
        "Name": "enum",
        "EnumValues": ["Misaligned", "Aligned", "Not
         mounted"]
      }
    }
  ]
}
],
"States": [
    {
  "Name": "Request Created",
  "DisplayName": "Created",
  "Description": "...",
  "PercentComplete": 20,
  "Style": "Success",
  "Transitions": [
```

```
        {
    "AllowedRoles": [],
    "AllowedInstanceRoles": ["Technician"],
    "Description": "...",
    "Function": "Start Wheel Alignment",
    "NextStates": [ "Aligning" ],
    "DisplayName": "Start Wheel Alignment"
  }
    ]
  },
  {
"Name": "Aligning",
"DisplayName": "Aligning",
"Description": "...",
"PercentComplete": 70,
"Style": "Success",
"Transitions": [
        {
    "AllowedRoles": [],
    "AllowedInstanceRoles": ["Car Owner"],
    "Description": "...",
    "Function": "SetTargetWheelAngle",
    "NextStates": ["Aligning"],
    "DisplayName": "Set TargetWheelAngle"
  },
        {
    "AllowedRoles": [],
    "AllowedInstanceRoles": ["Car Owner"],
    "Description": "...",
    "Function": "SetMode",
    "NextStates": ["Aligning"],
```

```
        "DisplayName": "Set Mode"
      }
    ]
  }
]
}
]
}
```

State Diagram

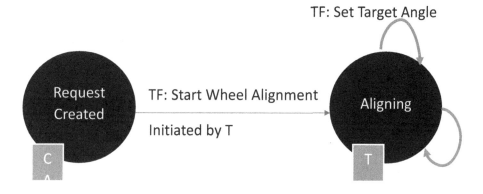

Fixing Pain Points

The solution is open to numerous alternatives; left to the reader's interpretation.

References to our version of implementation can be derived from the previous chapters, such as the BBChain View.

Index

A

Application architecture, 214
Architecture design
    factors, 196, 197
    fundamental process, 196
    on/off-chain combinations, 219
Azure
    Active Directory, 35
    business applications and
        presentation tools, 37
    components, 157
    metadata of existing
        information, 37
    process challenges, 37
    Workbench, 35
Azure Active Directory, 154
Azure Blockchain
        Workbench, 35–37
Azure CosmosDB, 170
Azure key vault, 74, 154
Azure Marketplace, Truffle, 135
Azure Stack
    enterprise ecosystem, 177
    Ethereum, 180
    GHOSSTTT protocol, 177
    multi-node, 178
    proof of authority, 181, 182
    Quorum, 179

single-click deployment
        option, 177
    template, 178

B

Bill'U
    AI service, 235
    application side, 231
    Azure CosmosDB, 239
    B2B2C platform, 239
    blockchain features, 237
    conventional methods, 233
    current offline process, retail
        customer, 232
    development tracks, 231
    digitized bill, blockchains, 238
    end-to-end encryption, 231
    querying mechanism, 235
    transaction between users, 234
    validator node, 234
Bitcoin, 83, 84, 89
Blockchain as a service, 194
Blockchain ecosystem
    consensus mechanisms, 273
    data and transactions, 283
    energy allocation, 283
    gadgets, 284
    hybrid chain, 282

© Shilpa Karkeraa 2020
S. Karkeraa, *Unlocking Blockchain on Azure*,
https://doi.org/10.1007/978-1-4842-5043-3

C

Printed in the United States
By Bookmasters